Under a Starless Sky

A FAMILY'S ESCAPE FROM IRAN

BANAFSHEH SEROV

HACHETTE AUSTRALIA

Banafsheh Serov is donating a percentage of her royalties from the sale
of *Under a Starless Sky* to the Asylum Seeker Resource Centre
www.asrc.org.au

HACHETTE AUSTRALIA

Published in Australia and New Zealand in 2008
by Hachette Australia
(An imprint of Hachette Livre Australia Pty Limited)
Level 17, 207 Kent Street, Sydney NSW 2000
www.hachette.com.au

First published in 2007 as *Sorrow of my Native Land* by Banafsheh (Bonnie) Serov

National Library of Australia
Cataloguing-in-Publication data

Serov, Banafsheh.
Under a starless sky : a family's escape from Iran

978 0 7336 2291 5 (pbk.)

Serov, Banafsheh - Childhood and youth.
Refugee children - Iran - Biography.
Iranians - Biography.
Iran - History - 1979-1997.

955.0542092

Cover and text design by Sandy Cull, gogoGingko
Front cover photograph courtesy of Getty Images
Author photograph by Lorrie Graham
Typesetting by Bookhouse, Sydney
Typeset in 13/18 pt Mrs Eaves
Printed in Australia by Griffin Press, Adelaide

Hachette Livre Australia's policy is to use papers
that are natural, renewable and recyclable products
and made from wood grown in sustainable forests.
The logging and manufacturing processes are expected
to conform to the environmental regulations
of the country of origin.

In memory of my grandmother

This is the story of my family's journey. A journey so long ago that time has slowly eroded people's features and names in our minds.

At times I've given permission for my imagination to take over where memories could no longer serve, because I don't believe facts should get in the way of telling a good story.

The Revolution

PREVIOUS PAGE: *Nina and Kamal, 1966*

Demonstrations in Tehran

My story begins on 8 September 1978. It was a hot, cloudless day and our family was spending the weekend at the Caspian Sea. Uncle Jalal sat behind the wheel of his new speedboat, slicing through the waves, spraying foamy water against our tanned skins.

Behind the boat, suspended like an umbilical cord, Dad bounced over the waves on a pair of water skis, his gold chain bobbing up and down against his chest. Dad bent his knees, turned his skis slightly to the left and changed direction till he was at a forty-five degree angle to the boat. He took one of his hands off the handlebar and waved. Then he changed hands, crouched low and extended his right arm to help him go faster. He flashed a big smile when he got to the other side and waved again. I clapped, impressed by his one-handed water skiing.

Dad took pride in his looks, always keeping up to date with fashion. His brown eyes, tall frame and easy smile were often compared to Omar Sharif. I watched him bounce over the waves, feeling proud to be his daughter and wishing his work as a partner of an accountancy firm and a lecturer at Tehran University did not absorb so much of his time.

Uncle Jalal made a U-turn. Dad bent his knees to change direction, lost control and crashed headfirst into the sea. The speedboat turned again and slowed as we got closer to him. He was laughing as he paddled awkwardly to retrieve his ski.

'One more time before we break for lunch,' he said to Uncle Jalal.

I was about to throw him the line when I noticed Mum waving at the edge of the water. Her other hand was firmly holding on to my brother's arm. Behzad, with his floaties still on, was struggling to set himself free.

Mum's arm continued to fan over her head. Watching her on the beach, I thought she looked almost frail. Helen, Uncle Jalal's wife, had joined her. She carried her baby Sabrina on her right hip. Her eldest daughter, Salomeh, stood beside her wrapped in a beach towel. Both women were waving for us to get back.

'I wonder what's happened?' Dad asked, puzzled.

'Nothing's happened.' Uncle Jalal winked. 'You know women. They probably have lunch ready and want us to hurry back before it gets cold.'

Closer to the shore, I jumped off the boat and swam the short distance to the beach while Dad helped Uncle Jalal anchor. I walked to where Mum was holding onto Behzad. She wore a yellow halter-neck dress she had bought on our recent holiday to Greece. Over her hair she wore a small blue scarf to protect her streaks from the sun. Her brown eyes were panicked, her face pale despite her summer tan. She stroked my face absentmindedly while watching the men secure the boat.

'Take your brother back to the villa,' Mum said, placing Behzad's struggling fist into mine. 'I need to speak to your father.' I stood dripping, while she picked up a towel with manicured fingers, shook the sand off, and walked towards the boat.

Uncle Jalal and Helen's villa overlooked the beach. I could have easily pulled Behzad the short distance there. But I stalled, wanting to know what had rattled Mum.

'I want to go back in the water,' Behzad protested. His small mouth pursed tight as tears began to well behind his long eyelashes. Behzad at six, three years younger than I, with his large dark eyes and round cheeks reminded me of a cherub in our storybooks. I felt sorry for him and loosened my grip a little, but not enough to set him free.

Mum stood next to Helen at the edge of the water where they waited for their men. 'Kamal, there's been trouble in Tehran.' Mum's voice trembled as she handed Dad the towel.

'What's happened?'

'The boy who delivered our bread from the village said martial law has been declared.'

'What for?'

Uncle Jalal joined them after securing the boat. He took Sabrina, who was stretching her round fingers towards him, from Helen. She squealed as Uncle Jalal pressed her against his wet skin.

'There have been demonstrations in Tehran against the Shah,' Helen said.

Uncle Jalal's eyes widened. 'Who were the demonstrators?'

'It's not clear. It could be the communists or the fundamentalists...who knows?' Helen waved her hand about her face dramatically as she spoke.

'What else?' Uncle Jalal said, his brown eyes losing all the lustre of the past few hours on the boat.

'They're demonstrating around the university and Jaleh Square,' Mum said in a tight voice. 'The army has opened fire on the unarmed people.' She paused. 'The boy said the streets are painted red with blood.'

There had been demonstrations in Iran since the beginning of January, but until now those events had almost no bearing on our lives in Tehran.

Dad's eyebrows gathered in creases at the bridge of his nose. He pressed his index finger on them as if suppressing a sharp pain. 'Nina, get the children ready,' he said with a tense jaw, 'we'll leave right away.'

'But we've made lunch,' Helen protested. The other three stared at her, Jalal with a mixture of embarrassment and annoyance. Dad closed his eyes and pressed at his temples. When he opened his eyes again there was great sadness in him.

Then Mum cradled Dad's face in her hands and smiled reassuringly. 'Helen's right, Kamal. We've made *Abeh Goosht*, it would be a shame to waste it.'

'What about the martial law?' he said, pulling her hands away.

'Lunch won't take long,' she said in a soothing voice. 'And we'll leave straight after.' She took Dad's hand and squeezed it gently. 'Come.'

Uncle Jalal and the others followed. My parents stopped when they reached Behzad and me. Dad bent over and kissed my forehead as he wrapped his towel around me. His lips felt cool. Mum gently took Behzad's hand in hers and this time he did not struggle.

We walked the short distance to the house in silence. From above, an observer would have mistaken our bent posture for a family retiring after an exhausting day at the beach.

At the villa we had our lunch on the shady veranda. We had spread a *sofreh* on the tiled floor around which our two families sat cross-legged. Uncle Jalal was inside phoning colleagues about the situation in Tehran. Dad had a shortwave radio close to his ear, straining to hear the newsreader between the static.

Salomeh and I were given the task of setting the food while Sabrina cooed happily in her bassinette and Behzad raced his 'hot wheel' cars. In the middle of the *sofreh* we placed some lavash bread, *torshi*, feta, *sabzi* and bottles of Coca-Cola. From the kitchen, the smell of the *Abeh Goosht* — lamb shanks and potatoes basking in turmeric — wafted in with the warm afternoon breeze.

Mum carried a large ceramic bowl filled with the stock from the *Abeh Goosht*. She placed it gently on the *sofreh*, careful not to spill any. The kids helped in making the *tilit* by cutting the lavash bread into bite-size pieces and throwing them into the bowl. Once enough bread had soaked the stock, the *tilit* was ready to be served.

Uncle Jalal came and sat cross-legged next to Dad. His eyes had lost their laughter. 'Some demonstrators have been killed,' he said. 'Not clear how many at this stage.'

'What did they say about the martial law?' Dad asked.

'Tehran is one of the eleven cities where the Shah has declared martial law. The curfew is set at 9 pm.'

It was 2.30 pm.

Mum served us lunch, trying to maintain a sense of normality. She served the men first, then us and Helen, then finally herself. After we all had some of the *tilit*, the de-boned lamb, potatoes, red beans and chickpeas were placed back into the ceramic bowl. Uncle Jalal, using a *goosht koob*, mashed the lot into a paste. This, along with any *torshi* or *sabzi*, we spooned from our plates into bite-size lavash cones.

Usually the midday meal was a time of great excitement. We sat cross-legged around the *sofreh* – women gossiped, men discussed business and we children fought over our favourite parts of the meat. All the food was placed in the middle, like steaming ships, for everyone to share and there was always enough for second and third helpings. Once the main meal was over we would lounge around, picking from plates of fruit and dates stuffed with walnuts. Adults usually enjoyed a hot cup of black tea prepared from a nearby samovar before falling asleep in the shady verandas.

On the day of the demonstrations, the silence around the *sofreh* was only interrupted by Behzad's zooming noises as he raced his toy cars.

We left as soon as the lunch dishes were washed. We stopped briefly at our own villa, making sure everything was locked, turning off the electricity and throwing away perishable foods. In the traffic heading away from the Caspian coast, Mum and Dad were silent in their thoughts.

Kandevan Tunnel

The Kandevan tunnel is halfway between the Caspian Sea and Tehran, through the Alborz mountains, which run along the northern part of Iran from Azarbaijan in the west to the Afghan border in the east. The Chaloos Road from Tehran to the Caspian Sea winds up the mountain to the Kandevan tunnel and then winds back down the other side. A traveller taking this road for the first time coming from the dry, smog-trapped air of Tehran would be surprised to find a lush and fertile land with humid air on the Caspian side of the mountain.

The Kandevan tunnel gets its name from the village of Kandevan near Tabriz. The people from this village live in cave-like dwellings and are well known for their rock-cutting craftsmanship. In the 1920s the Kandevan villagers cut a tunnel through solid rocks in the Alborz mountains. It is only wide enough to allow vehicles to move in one direction at a time along a single road.

A traffic light at the mouth of the tunnel determined which direction could go. People used this waiting time to climb out of their overcrowded cars and stretch their legs. As we drew closer, we saw that the traffic stretched for miles down the winding Chaloos Road.

'Oh my god, look at this traffic, Nina.' Dad stuck his head out the window to get a better look. All around us people were climbing out of their cars, the anxiety of wanting to get home clear in their eyes. Most smoked, taking long deliberate drags from their cigarettes. They threw the butts carelessly into the green bushes and the rain later washed them downstream to settle on the patchwork rice fields at the foot of the mountain.

The clock on the dashboard blinked 5.50 pm.

'Damn. At this rate, it could take us hours before we get home.' Dad switched off the engine and rolled down his window, turning to look at us. Beside me, Behzad was asleep; he held his old foam pillow with its jagged edges close to his chest. Dad smiled. Behzad had refused time and time again to give up his pillow in favour of a new one.

'Let's have a cigarette, Kamal,' Mum pulled a packet of Rothmans from her handbag and stepped out of the car. They leaned on the bonnet, close together. Dad cupped his hand around the gold lighter to first light Mum's and then his own cigarette. The sun hung low in the sky, throwing peach-coloured rays across the sea of cars. There was a faint smell of lamb and chicken kebab in the air. It all seemed far removed from the tense eyes of the travellers around us.

'Kamal, look! Something's happening.' Mum stood, straining her neck. 'I think there's a fight.'

I stood up and squeezed myself through the sunroof to get a better look.

Ten cars ahead of us, in front of a vendor selling kebabs, two men, one in his late teens and the other middle-aged, were having a heated argument. A crowd was building around them. A frail old woman was pleading with the younger man to come away with her. She pulled at his sleeve. It seemed to work, but then the older man said something and the other man punched him, sending him flying into the middle of the road. A car coming from the opposite direction swerved to miss him.

The older man picked himself up and flew into a rage. He ran to his car throwing off two men who tried to stop him. He climbed into a car behind us and seconds later came out waving a butcher's knife. Behind him, a woman called out, 'For the love of God, Asghar! He's only a boy. Please...let him go.'

'Get back into the car, woman,' Asghar spat out.

'Asghar...please.'

'I said get back in the car.'

A few men tried to hold Asghar back by grabbing his arms. But Asghar was strong and freed himself easily. His bloodshot eyes scanned the crowd for his victim, his nostrils flaring. He saw him hiding behind a white Renault and the younger man ran, weaving between cars and pushing people out of his way. Asghar chased after him waving his knife in the air, and threatening anyone who tried to stop him. Some men, fearful of their wives and children getting hurt, pushed them back into their cars. The children, curious at what was happening, were slow to move which resulted in a clip to the back of their heads from their parents. A woman close to us was shouting for someone to stop the fight before it ended in bloodshed. Others were running to get the police who were directing the traffic at the tunnel's entrance. Car horns blasted all around us and it all added to the general hysteria. Cars coming in the opposite direction slowed down to a crawl causing drivers behind them to lean on their car horns. The young man suddenly changed direction and ran towards our car. Asghar, tired by the chase, was slower to react.

Dad threw his half-smoked cigarette away. Mum, stunned, was glued to where she stood. Dad pushed her towards the passenger door. 'Nina, get into the car...Get down from there,' he pointed at me. 'Roll up your windows and lock the doors.' Dad climbed back in and did the same. He had one hand on the ignition key and the other on the gear stick. His shoulders tensed.

Behzad, blinked awake, dazed, wondering what all the commotion was about. 'What's going on? Are we nearly home?' No one answered him.

Outside, the younger man was almost at our car. He turned to see how far ahead he was when he tripped and fell. He stretched out his arms to break his fall, and landed on our bonnet.

Mum screamed. The boy looked up. His black hair, wet with sweat, was stuck to his forehead. At that moment, Asghar reached our car as well, his wife running behind him, screaming and pleading with him to stop. The boy rolled onto his back just as Asghar caught up with him. He tried getting up, but his feet kept slipping, throwing him back on our bonnet. In desperation he rolled across the bonnet and fell between our car and the mountain.

Asghar followed, his knife raised high over his head.

'Close your eyes . . . don't look,' Dad yelled at us. He turned the ignition. The engine roared into life. Ahead of us the tunnel's light had turned green and the traffic had started to move a little. I pulled Behzad's face onto my lap. I bent over him, with my arms folded over our heads. Outside a woman screamed above the roar of the engine.

'Asghaaaaaaaaaaarrrrrrrr . . .'

Dad pressed his palm on the horn and kept it there. Our wheels screeched. The car swerved, throwing Behzad and I off our seats. The tyres fought to keep their grip on the road. The nauseating smell of petrol and burning rubber filled the car. Behzad and I were pressed in the leg space between the driver's and backseats. Gravel crunched beneath our wheels just before we stopped and the engine hummed as if catching its breath. Neither Behzad nor I got up from where we had fallen. My head felt like shattered glass. For what seemed a long time, no one spoke.

I waited until I no longer smelled burning rubber, 'Daddy, can we get up now?'

'Yes, sweetheart. It's okay.'

We sat up. Behzad, startled, started to cry. He climbed over the seats to find security in the soft roundness of Mum's arms.

He buried his head in the crook of her neck, breathing in her comfort.

We had stopped on the other side of the road, not far from where we were originally. The cars were travelling slowly into the tunnel, their passengers looking curiously at us.

Mum, with Behzad wrapped around her, held her head in her hand. Her shoulders were shaking. Dad placed one hand on her shoulder and handed her a tissue. She blew her nose loudly. 'Did you see their faces, Kamal?'

Dad remained silent. He rolled down his window and lit another cigarette. He put the car into first gear and with some difficulty pushed his way back into the moving traffic. A car beeped, annoyed at being forced to give way.

When the traffic stopped again we could see the red traffic light at the tip of the Kandevan Tunnel. Dad turned off the engine. Mum's crying had subsided into a sniffle. She looked out of the window with unfocused eyes. Dad pressed his temples. All of a sudden, he opened the door and got out.

'Where are you going?' Mum called after him.

'I'll be back soon,' Dad answered over his shoulder.

There were police stations on both sides of the Kandevan Tunnel to direct the cars. The traffic police, with white caps and whistles, ensured the cars entered the tunnel one at a time and they stopped drivers from running the red light.

Kamal walked up to an officer issuing a fine to an unco-operative driver.

'Officer, I want to report a possible murder,' Kamal interrupted.

The officer looked up, annoyed. 'What murder?'

'There was a fight and one of the men pulled a knife and...'

'Okay, okay,' the officer put his palms up to stop Kamal going any further. 'You need to see the sergeant over there,' he said sharply and turned his attention back to the offending driver.

Kamal drew a deep breath through his nose to control his anger and walked to where a group of twenty people had gathered around a heavily built man in a dark blue police uniform. As he drew closer, he saw the young man who had been in the fight. He looked unharmed, but his white shirt was caked with mud and there were streaks running down his dirty face. Kamal noticed the boy's eyes were puffed, as if stung by bees, and a faint odour of dried urine clung to his clothes.

Standing next to the sergeant were Asghar and his wife. Asghar stood silent with downcast eyes. His heavy frame, tired by the physical exertion, sagged above his belt. A dark patch, the colour of bruised fruit, had formed above his left eye. His wife stood beside him, whimpering while she spoke.

'I swear on the Koran, my husband is a good man.' She lifted Asghar's chin up with her cupped hands so everyone could see his face. 'Look what this boy did to him,' she said, pointing to the other man. 'Anyone in my husband's place would lose their temper.' She searched the faces crowded around her for approval. Some bystanders nodded in agreement, enjoying being the jury in this open-air courtroom.

The young man was talking rapidly to the sergeant who was trying to slow him down. 'As Allah is my witness, this man here tried to kill me... He's a lunatic... If it wasn't for his wife, I'd be dead now.'

'But *Alham-du-LeAllah*,' the sergeant said, eager for a quick resolution, 'you're all right and there's been no great harm done. You yourself have not been completely guiltless,' he said, shaking his index finger at the young man. 'So, come now, do the right brotherly thing. Kiss and make up.' The sergeant extended his arms to bring the two parties together.

'But...' the young man began to protest.

'No buts!' the sergeant retorted impatiently. 'Can't you see the traffic building up? Come. Kiss and make up and get back to your cars...That's a good lad...And stop making any more trouble for me.'

With a wave of his hand, the sergeant beckoned the men to kiss one another on both cheeks and dismissed the crowd. Reluctantly, the people around them slowly dispersed.

Kamal walked back to the car, smiling and shaking his head as if enjoying a private joke. The lights had just turned green and he had to run the last few steps to make it to the car in time.

The cars behind him beeped their horns impatiently as Dad dived back into the car.

'What happened to you?' Mum asked, narrowing her eyes, puzzled by the expression on his face.

'I went to report the incident back there.'

She sat up, 'And?'

'They were both already there. Suffice to say, the problem was solved in the good ol' Iranian way.' He flashed her a knowing smile.

We didn't get back to Tehran until well past midnight, and were only stopped once. The soldier had shone his torch at Mum and Dad's tanned faces and us sleeping in the backseat, then waved the car through. We climbed into our beds gratefully, not realising we had just had our first taste of the chaos that was about to rule our lives.

Marg bar America!

We lived in the northern and more affluent part of Tehran, in a white four-storey building. From our kitchen window we could see Damavand, the snow-capped peak of the Alborz Mountain. Mum designed the interior, ensuring all the bedrooms and balconies overlooked the small manicured garden in the middle of the front yard. As was customary in Iran, our front yard was separated from the street by a two-metre-high iron gate. We lived in the first storey with Mamman, my paternal grandmother. Dad's eldest sister, Mahin, with her husband, Salman, and their children lived on the second floor of the building. Dad's other sister, Shahin, and her husband, Shapoor, with their children were on the third. Akbar, an old childhood friend of Dad's from Tabriz, lived on the top floor with his wife and young son.

Since the demonstrations, there had been an increasing number of strikes in the oil industry, the post office, government factories, and banks. Subsequent protest marches had led to more killings and the Shah's martial law was still in force. Despite the ongoing unrest, our school opened as usual in late September. Kooros was a bilingual primary school based on the British school system. Both Behzad and I had started there from kindergarten. It was one of the new international schools which had sprung up to cater for the growing number of English and American children in Iran. The affluent and Western-educated Iranians fought hard against one another for the few spots available to them, and were willing to pay the high fees demanded, to send their children to the same schools.

After our summer holidays there was a noticeable absence of most of the foreign and some of the Iranian students who had fled with their families as a result of the fighting and the anti-Western sentiments. As a precaution, Dad's driver Ali took us to school. Ali was from the poorer southern Tehran and used to play tapes in the car. These were black market revolutionary tapes, recordings of speeches from mullahs made around Iran over the past few months against the Shah's regime, handed out by university students and clerics at Friday sermons. The tapes were poor quality, which made it hard to understand the words but the mullahs kept talking about the same person: Ayatollah Khomeini. I asked Ali who the Ayatollah was.

'Ayatollah Khomeini is our Imam,' he said passionately. 'He is sent by Allah to save us from this tyrannical regime.'

I stared at him blankly. I wanted to ask more, but the people on the tape started screaming. A voice shouted, 'The soldiers are here!' There were sounds of gunshots. Women screamed and children cried for their mothers. There was a flurry of footsteps as people rushed to get out.

It sounded like some fell and were trampled.

I could make out chanting: 'Marg bar Shah ... Marg bar America ... Death to Shah ... Death to America.' The chants were drowned out by the rat-tat-tat of guns. Glass shattered and people were crying out. The tape recorder continued recording, turning calmly despite the chaos around it. Then somewhere close to the tape machine there was a hissing sound. Those who had remained in the mosque began to cough. The coughing grew louder. Someone called out, 'My eyes ... [cough] ... my throat ... [more coughing] ... I can't see a thing.'

Footsteps fled past the forgotten recorder, knocking it over. I could make out people chanting outside the mosque, bursts of gunfire, and screams of people as they scattered throughout the mosque. Then all became silent as the tape ran out.

We heard those tapes often on the way to school. Behzad would sit quietly in the backseat and stare out the window, but at nights he rocked in his bed and woke up with nightmares.

Over the next few months, we became curiously used to the sound of gunfire. Our quiet streets were at times punctured by the sound of bullets. I found a bullet shell half-embedded into our back patio and kept it for good luck.

Most of the fighting was concentrated in the older, southern part of Tehran. This is where the bazaars, mosques, cemetery and Tehran University were located. It was also the poorer, more congested part of the city. Geographically it is a two-hour drive from Qom, the religious centre of Iran, where the seeds of the revolution were first planted.

In 1953, Dr Muhammad Mossadeq, the democratically elected Prime Minister of Iran, had been overthrown by a CIA-backed coup. Mossadeq had outraged the West by nationalising Iran's profitable Anglo-Iranian oil company. At the time the British employees of the oil company lived in fenced off compounds in large air-conditioned houses, while the Iranians working for them lived in squalor and were paid a pittance. Mossadeq requested a 50/50 share of the profits and proposed that the monarchy, the Shah, should act as a figurehead rather than a ruler. The young Shah fled the country with his first wife Soraya. Mossadeq's actions prompted the aging Churchill to convince Eisenhower to instigate 'Operation Ajax' which resulted in Mossadeq's overthrow. Many Iranians believe that had Mossadeq been successful, Iran would have become a democracy. Over the next two decades, the consequences of the coup, and subsequent reinstatement of Mohammad Reza Shah Pahlavi, the Shah, to the throne, left a deep distrust of American foreign policy in the Iranian psyche. Since then, there had been a few uprisings in Iran, but they had no leadership or direction.

In 1976, Amnesty International accused SAVAK (the Shah's CIA trained secret police) of torturing 3000 mostly political prisoners and announced that Iran's human rights record was one of the worst in the world. During the Shah's reign, SAVAK had gained a reputation as the most notorious and murderous institution in the Middle East. Fear of SAVAK discouraged any discussion of politics, particularly if it was anti-Shah. It was rumoured SAVAK informers were in every school and business. Many who did speak against the Shah were never seen or heard from again.

In 1978 the hatred and anger finally erupted. In Khomeini the people found a leader and in Islam a direction. Initially Khomeini's supporters were university students discontented with the widening income gap, the lack of social justice and the 'Status of Forces Agreement' between the Shah and the USA which gave immunity to the Americans living in Iran against acts punishable under its laws. The peasants and the urban poor fuelled by Friday sermons in their mosques were also willing to face army tanks in defiance of the Shah's lack of religious following and the increased Western modernisation. In a futile attempt to rebuild some of the royal family's Islamic piety and to stop the demonstrations, the Shah had ordered the closure of casinos and gambling clubs. He had also dismissed or imprisoned officials (including his prime minister) in high government posts under corruption charges. Dr Aram, Mum's boss from the Ministry of Health, was amongst those imprisoned.

As the revolution gained momentum and killings escalated, secular intellectuals, socialists and nationalists, whom until then had remained neutral in what they saw as a struggle between the Shah and the mullahs, joined the movement believing they were rising against fifty years of dictatorship. To the religious, Khomeini was Ali (Prophet Mohammad's son-in-law and Shia's highly revered first Imam), and to the secularists, Mossadeq.

By the beginning of December 1978, the whole country was paralysed by strikes. We had electricity and gas for only a few hours a day. There were long queues in front of petrol stations, with people and cars waiting for hours in the hope of filling their tanks and paraffin cans. Everything was becoming scarce.

Inflation was rife. Contacts became vital for getting household goods. A black market economy flourished for everything from American dollars to everyday commodities.

Despite the shortages, the mood on the street was one of unity and buoyant optimism. Upon coming into power in the 1920s, Reza Shah intolerant of religious hierarchy had banned the wearing of the turban for all except the most senior clergy. Additionally he had banned the wearing of the veil for women and had opened state schools to minimise the educational influences of *madrassas*. During the revolution more and more men grew facial hair and women wore the hejab, in visual defiance against the Shah's regime and its Westernised ideals.

Kamal looked at his dashboard. His petrol tank was showing half-empty.

'Damn!' he cursed under his breath. It was the second time this week his petrol tank had been drained. The worst thing was that it happened at his work's car park.

I should get someone to watch the cars all day, he thought. But anyone he hired could easily siphon a bit of petrol everyday from the cars and sell it on the black market for ten times the pump price. He had enough petrol for today. His main concern was the two empty paraffin containers he needed for heaters.

He turned into Pahlavi Street where he knew there was a petrol station. The queue was over a kilometre. One man stood with his four children, the youngest no older than seven or eight years old, each holding an empty container. The children's faces looked dark from layers of pollution and dirt. Their knees and elbows stuck out of their thin limbs like doorknobs. Kamal cursed again under his breath; this could take hours.

He drove past and double-parked his car at the front of the petrol station, where he had a clear view of the queue. He turned off his engine and watched a man and woman fill up two large paraffin cans. The man's face was almost fully covered by his bushy beard. He wore faded Levis and a khaki jacket that had seen better days. The woman's hair was covered and she wore a hand-knitted scarf around her neck. Their bare fingers were pink from hours of standing in the cold.

Once the cans were filled, the man placed a long stick across his back. The woman checked that the lids were secured tight and, with some difficulty, lifted each can onto the ends of the stick. The man's back hunched under the weight. Kamal pulled out his wallet and checked the contents, then opened the car door and stepped out, taking rapid steps towards the couple. The cold blast of winter stung his face. He buttoned up his overcoat.

The couple did not notice him at first so Kamal stepped into their path. 'How much for your paraffin?' he asked.

'It's not for sale,' the man retorted. His words were a little strained from the weight on his shoulders. He tried to step around Kamal who put a hand on the man's chest, 'I'll offer you 300 tomans for each container.' He knew it was twice what the man would have paid.

'I told you it's not for sale,' the man said, this time a little less forcefully. Kamal, sensing the man's willingness, quickly increased the price. 'Five hundred tomans. This is my final offer. Otherwise I'll offer it to the next person in line.'

The woman leaned over and whispered something in the man's ear. The man nodded. With her help, he placed his load carefully on the icy footpath, and stretched his back. At his full height, he stood taller than Kamal.

'I can only sell you one. I've got a sick baby and an elderly mother living in a rented room.' The man's face tightened. 'I haven't worked for months. I've had to borrow money to get this paraffin for our heater and a little bit of petrol for my motorbike so I can do some odd jobs.'

The man reminded Kamal of his younger brother Nasser. Kamal's expression softened. He nodded and turned his head so he didn't have to look at the embarrassment in the man's eyes. They swapped the empty container in the back of Kamal's car with the man's full one. Kamal then pulled out several petrol rations which he had bought on the black market.

'Here's 500 tomans, some petrol rations and my card. Come by my office, I might have a job for you in our car park.' As Kamal drove away he saw the couple in his rearview mirror with their heads bent forward together over the small card.

A few days later Kamal arrived late to the office. He was about to push open the large glass door when a man's voice stopped him.

'Agha Kamal!'

Kamal turned and looked at the tall man who had emerged from behind the leafless tree. It took him a few seconds to recognise the man from the petrol station.

'*Salaam*, Agha Kamal,' the man stepped forward, uncertain if he had been recognised. 'My name is Rashid. You remember from the other day? You said you might have a job for me.'

'Yes, of course I remember. I — I wasn't sure you'd be coming.'

'Well...' Rashid dropped his eyes, 'my wife and I never had a proper education. I took your card with me to the Friday prayers. Our mullah told me where to come.'

'I'm glad you did. Come inside.'

From that day onwards Rashid guarded the cars like a sheepdog guards his herd. He also made the tea, which meant he always knew what was being said as he moved around the office soundlessly, carrying fragrant jasmine teas and small lumps of sugars on large round trays.

Allah-O-Akbar

We sat cross-legged in neat lines according to our class. An unscheduled assembly had been announced in the hall on the third floor of our school. On days when it was raining, or too icy to play outside, the ten by twenty metre room doubled as our indoor playground. There were large windows at one end of the hall where we could look down onto the quiet street. Smaller windows at the opposite end provided plenty of light during the daytime. It was December and the walls were proudly decorated with the children's artwork and Christmas decorations. There was a dark patch where the photo of the Shah and his wife had once hung on the wall. No one knew who had pulled it down.

We all spoke excitedly amongst ourselves, happy to be excused from our afternoon classes. The teachers did little to quieten us. The noise finally subsided when the two principals walked in. In Iran it was mandatory for international businesses to have Iranian partners, which meant international schools had two principals.

Mrs Briggs, our English principal, walked up to the dais. She was a stocky woman with soft blue eyes which turned hard when handing out punishment for demerits. She blew her nose loudly on her white handkerchief and then tucked it into her sleeve. She waited until we were all quiet.

'Children, as you know there's been a lot of unrest in Tehran's streets lately. A lot of this aggression is towards Western businesses. We have decided that for the safety of our students we will be closing our school until further notice. Your parents will be notified with a letter we will be sending home with you today.'

The room was quiet. A shiver ran up my spine and I shuddered involuntarily. I looked around and saw the news slowly sinking in for the older children. A few of the girls started to cry. We were dismissed back to our classes. The younger classes were lead out in two straight lines. Behzad stood with his year one class. He flashed me a smile, revealing two missing front teeth. He waved as their class was led away by their teacher.

Back in our classroom, our teacher was bombarded with questions. 'Does this mean we don't have a school any more?'

'No, it just means that while the streets are unsafe you will have to stay home.' Her voice was calm and cool like a light summer breeze.

'Are they going to bomb our school?' This time she paled a little. A strand of silky black hair had escaped from her hairclip. She pulled the clip out, pinned the strand of hair back into place and looked up at the student who had asked the question.

'I hope not.' There was a slight tremble in her voice.

Since the demonstrations had begun there had been deliberate attacks and firebombing of banks which dealt with international companies, liquor shops and cinemas — anything that symbolised the West. International schools had received bomb threats and recently we had rocks and bricks, followed by abuse, hurled at us from over the school wall.

None of us had been allowed to go to the movies since August when 377 people were killed in a cinema fire in Abadan. The attackers had locked the exit doors, trapping the victims inside. Rumours spread that SAVAK had caused the fire.

For the next few months my cousins and I spent our days playing in the rubble behind our house where developers had abandoned their ambitions. The thick snow that covered the piled dirt made for a perfect playground. At night we huddled around gaslights listening to our parents talk about the revolution in hushed tones, or we all listened to the BBC World Service between bursts of static. The adults listened to the news with worried expressions and talked about what might become of our school. Mum was especially worried about Behzad who was rocking in his sleep and waking up from nightmares.

Meanwhile, outside on the rooftops of Tehran, a revolution of a different kind was taking place.

Traditionally, in neighbourhoods all around Iran, the young men blessed with strong voices would go on rooftops to call the faithful to prayer.

In Tehran, this was mainly practised in the southern parts, which were more religious. In our street, an old man with memories of a once angelic voice would faithfully climb the steps up to his roof at dusk. He would warm his vocal cords with honey-sweetened tea. He cupped one hand with its protruding purple veins close to his mouth. He drew the night air into his lungs and called out to the faithful.

'Allah-O-Akbar . . . Allah-O-Akbar,' his words filled the evening. I grew up listening to the rise and fall of his calling, often as I was drifting off to sleep. In my bed, under layers of blanket or with the sweet smell of jasmine flowers wafting through my window, his calling was like a lullaby. My breathing would slow down to match its rhythm: 'Allah-O-Akbar. God is great. Allah-O-Akbar.'

From the beginning of the revolution in September 1978, others responded to his calling. At first it was a mere handful of people. By December the night air was filled with voices rising and falling in harmony long after the red glow of the setting sun had made way for the blanket of darkness.

Upstairs at Mahin's, Kamal and the other men were gathered around the dining table, drinking whisky and trying to outdo one another with their insights on the revolution. A gas lamp in the middle of the room threw a soft golden glow on the walls, while a battery-operated shortwave radio was tuned into the BBC news.

'In Paris, the Iranian dissident mullah Ayatollah Khomeini has once again urged his countrymen to join the uprising. In a stirring speech the charismatic Ayatollah has vowed to release his country from the tyranny of the West. He has continued to denounce the Shah as an American puppet. Meanwhile in Iran, thousands of demonstrators are pouring daily into the streets. Iran's newly appointed Prime Minister Bakhtiar has had no influence in easing the tension. Iran's military is reported to be losing hundreds of men as soldiers are defecting daily to join the revolution . . .'

Kamal and the other three men, Salman, Shapoor and Akbar, crowded around the table with a bottle of Johnnie Walker between them. Their faces were flushed from the warmth of the alcohol. The women sat on wooden chairs, talking amongst themselves.

Kamal looked at his mother sitting on the couch and listening with detached interest. Once in a while she would bite down on her lower lip, cluck her tongue and shake her head in dismay.

He became agitated. He switched off the radio, 'All we do is talk.'

His sister Mahin gave a guttural laugh. 'What did you expect to do? Run in front of guns?'

He stared at her for what seemed a long time. When he spoke again his voice sounded stuck in his throat. 'People are dying in the streets and we sit in our cosy apartments and talk of revolution.' He brushed his hair back with his hands, lacing his fingers behind his neck and keeping his eyes fixed on the flame flickering inside the gas lamp.

Through the shut windows a faint call of *Allah-O-Akbar* could be heard. Everyone listened to the sounds that had become so familiar. Kamal placed the palms of his hands on the table and pushed himself up. He looked at Mahin. 'You're right. I might not have the courage to step in front of a bullet, but at least I can be a part of what's going on out there,' he pointed in the direction of the street.

Flicking through old *LIFE* magazines with our flashlights, my cousin Zoya and I were unaware of the commotion that had started in the living room. As the sounds grew louder, we stopped and listened. We stepped out to the hallway, and in the faint glow of the gas lamp, we saw the men putting on their jackets, a little unsteady on their feet.

'You can't go in your condition,' Mum spoke with suppressed anger. 'You're going to kill yourself falling off the roof.'

Dad squared his shoulders and walked out, not bothering to close the door behind him. We heard his boots stepping heavily on the concrete stairs. Encouraged by Dad the other men followed, feeling their way up the dark stairwell. The women stared at the open door as if expecting them to come back any minute.

Mamman bit down on her lip. 'Nina, why didn't you stop them?'

'Mamman, you saw them. There was nothing I could do.'

'At least go up after them. Make sure they don't fall over the edge,' her voice trembled. Mum looked at her. Mamman's eyes were glassy with tears. Mum took Mamman's old hands into hers and her daughters put their arms reassuringly around her. Ever since she had lost her husband eight years ago, Mamman's children had protected her, as if guarding a fragile china doll.

'I'll make sure they're all right,' Mum tried to sound confident as she reached for her jacket.

On the roof the men stood and listened. Voices were rising and falling in unison from almost every rooftop. It had started to snow. The snowflakes floated gracefully from the black sky, melting quickly as they hit the concrete. In the morning the sharp edges of the buildings would be buried under the white round curves.

Kamal looked up, inviting the flakes to his face. The air was crisp. A large lump choked his throat. He closed his eyes, breathing in the night air. The cold had helped clear his head and sharpen his senses. His heart thundered in his ears. He thought about one of his American employees at Deloitts. Almost all of their international staff had left the company; John, however, could not be persuaded to leave. 'Leave, Kamal? Are you crazy? Look around you. History is being made right in front of our eyes. I'd never forgive myself if I leave here for the comfort of white picket fences back home.'

A thin smiled formed on Kamal's lips at the memory. John was right, this was history in the making and Kamal wanted to be part of it. He wanted to be part of the movement started by Mossadeq all those years ago. He opened his eyes and found the other three men staring at him.

'Why aren't you joining in?' asked Shapoor, slurring his words a little.

Kamal stared out to where the voices were coming from. He breathed in the cold air and cried out his first *Allah-O-Akbar* just as a tear escaped from the corner of his eye and ran quickly down his face.

Mum stayed with Dad on the roof for most of that night. From my bedroom I could see small pinpricks of light on rooftops all over our neighbourhood as other people climbed on their roofs as well.

The *Allah-O-Akbars* I could hear outside had a sense of urgency and the tones were angry and defiant. Sitting on my bed, with my knees drawn to my chest, I felt scared. The night call no longer sounded like a comforting lullaby. I didn't understand that for my parents this was their voice of objection. All I knew was that another pillar of security and comfort for me had been dismantled, and I wept for the loss.

First demonstration

December 10th is the holy day of Ashura. In November, in an attempt to regain control, the Shah had declared religious demonstrations illegal. On 9 December the BBC had announced that the ban was lifted for the holy day of Ashura.

Kamal and Nina woke up early. In the car Nina warmed her hands close to the car's heater.

'How many people are they expecting today?' she asked Kamal.

'I'm not sure. Rumour has it there are going to be a few thousand.'

Up ahead the traffic had slowed as each car was stopped at a barricade. Some cars turned around, but most were waved through. When they reached the barricade a soldier flagged them over. Kamal rolled down his window. The cold wind slapped his face.

'Where are you going?' The soldier looked in his twenties. His breath smelt of cheap cigarettes. His accent and dark skin

placed him from the southern part of Iran, close to the Persian
Gulf. He had pulled up the collar of his khaki jacket to protect
his ears against the chill and his machine gun hung loosely on
a shoulder strap by his side.

'We're going south,' Kamal's voice sounded as if rising from
a dried well. He cleared his throat.

'Are you aware there are going to be demonstrations
today?'

'Yes, we are.'

The soldier pushed back his cap and leaned his face through
the car window, his voice weary with long hours at his post.
'Agha, you realise you probably will not be able to come back
tonight?'

'Yes, we are,' Kamal answered without hesitating. His eyes
locked on the soldier's. The soldier straightened and pulled
his cap down tight over his ears. 'Okay then,' and he waved
them through.

As soon as they passed the barricade, Nina reached into her
handbag and pulled out a black scarf she had borrowed from
her mother. She placed the folded scarf over her head and
drew the ends into a tight knot under her chin. She wore no
make-up or jewellery and had a defiant look in her eyes. She
caught Kamal looking at her with a soft expression.

They parked the car in an alleyway and followed the crowd
towards the amplified voices in the distance. They walked in
quick steps, half-running. By now the sun had risen high in
the sky. The snow of a few days ago had all but melted, leaving
behind an icy residue blackened by dirt and pollution. 'Death
to Shah' and 'Death to America' were graffitied on nearby

buildings. The shell of a burnt car stood as a reminder of the events of the past few months.

Nina and Kamal reached the demonstrators after walking for almost a kilometre. All along the tree-lined avenue people walked side by side with fists punching the air. The men were unshaven and the women wore the hejab. There was no beginning and no end, just a sea of people dressed in black with voices that cracked like thunder along the tree-lined street.

'*Marg bar Shah*! Death to Shah.'

'*Khomeini Rahbar*. Khomeini's our leader!'

Above the crowd a military helicopter hovered. Reporters had climbed the trees, taking pictures that would be on the front page of every international newspaper by the next morning.

Nina stared at the crowd with her mouth slightly open. She squeezed Kamal's arm. A couple broke away from the crowd, smiling as if greeting a close friend. The woman, carrying carnations in her hand, walked straight to one of the soldiers lined along the street. The soldier tensed, firming his grip on his rifle. He shot a nervous look at another soldier standing a few metres away from him. The woman pulled out a white carnation from her pile and slipped it in the nozzle of the rifle. The man accompanying her cupped the soldier's face in his hands and kissed each cheek as if welcoming a brother. Then they turned and disappeared back into the crowd.

Nina looked at the soldier, he was trying hard to blink back his tears. Then Kamal and Nina walked side by side into the middle of the crowd. Kamal's stomach felt as tight as a knot and a cold sweat hung to his back. He opened and closed his hand repeatedly by his side, but had not yet raised it above his head. Next to him, Nina had started chanting with the others, her small frame almost lost in the crowd. Her chin was raised up to the sky, her face streaked with tears. Kamal felt his heart pounding against his heavy coat.

Throughout his adult life, Kamal had conditioned himself to keep his political thoughts private. Since the beginning of the unrest he had become more vocal, but to openly demonstrate against the regime was still unthinkable. He lifted his face as if in prayer. He opened his mouth: 'Death to Shah.'

The words sounded like a whisper, hardly audible even to himself. He swallowed hard. His mouth was dry like sandpaper.

'Death to Shah.' This time it came out louder, stronger. He raised his fists self-consciously over his head. He punched the air hesitantly at first, but as his confidence grew he punched harder and chanted louder.

'Death to America! Death to Shah!'

Relief washed over him with every word. Each step further lifted the heavy burden he had carried in his heart for so many years. He wanted America, with its puppet dictator, out and an Iranian democratic government chosen by her people in.

They marched past the soldiers. Kamal watched demonstrators kissing, hugging and placing flowers in the soldiers' guns. He wanted to do the same. He gathered his strength and broke from the crowd. He walked up to a young soldier. In the soldier's face he saw the face of his son, his brother and his own youth. Tears streaked his face as he hugged the younger man.

'God be with you, brother,' the soldier responded.

—⚋—

Four and a half million people lived in Tehran and over a million walked in the Ashura demonstrations that day. They came together in one voice. They held hands and sang revolutionary songs. They carried one another's children on their shoulders. They held up banners with revolutionary slogans. Thousands carried pictures of Ayatollah Khomeini which until then had been illegal.

They walked with the belief that change had come; that Iran would finally be the master of her own destiny. They could taste freedom of speech and became high on it. The military took passive interest in the demonstrations. Each day more and more soldiers defected from the Shah's army and joined their countrymen in the movement.

The Shah has fled

On 16 January 1979 Kamal sat in his office behind a large mahogany desk. A cigarette burned in the ashtray next to him. On the wall a single nail which once held a picture of the Shah stood naked. Kamal had pulled down the Shah's picture the day after the Ashura demonstrations. He had felt a weight lift off his shoulders as he'd climbed up on a wooden chair and taken it down. He rested his forehead in his hand as he scanned his paperwork.

Outside, a commotion had started in the street. As if on cue, all the drivers started beeping their horns. Kamal lifted his head and looked in the direction of the window. He dropped his pen on the table and was about to walk to the window when Azim burst into the room. 'Shah's gone! His plane just took off for Egypt.'

Kamal's heart pounded hard. He walked to the window and pressed his palms against the glass and stared down at the scene below with disbelief. The corners of his mouth slowly turned up into a wide smile.

'My god, it's true. He's gone.' Kamal turned away from the window and pulled his jacket off the back of his seat. He pushed past Azim, slapping his friend on the back. 'He's gone, Azim. This time for good!'

The office was almost deserted. A few staff were still in the building kissing and congratulating one another. One of the secretaries, a well-dressed woman in her mid-thirties, sat behind her desk with her head in her hands. Her shoulders were shaking under her silk shirt.

Kamal didn't stop to talk to anyone as he ran down the flight of stairs to the street. The roads were jammed with vehicles and people. All the cars had their wipers standing upright, waving from side to side. People were shouting slogans, 'Death to Shah, Death to America, Death to Carter', but their voices were drowned out by the noise from the celebrations. Children ran in between the crowds waving sparklers, their sparks trailing behind them. From every building people threw confetti and rose petals down at the crowds. Patriotic anthems blared loudly from people's radios. Kamal had never seen such outpouring of excitement and celebration. The sound of the horns was deafening. People danced on top of cars and in the middle of the road. Kamal stood there, allowing it all to wash over him.

He thought of his *TIME* magazines that arrived torn or blackened with ink whenever there were any articles against the Shah or Iran.

No more, he thought. He's gone.

He loosened the tie that felt like a noose around his neck and started to walk with the crowd towards the university. On the way strangers hugged him, women offered him flowers and sweets, and children danced around him. People hung posters of Ayatollah Khomeini from their buildings. All over Iran statues of the Shah and his father were pulled down. It was the end of the 'Peacock Throne' which had begun in 1925.

A man was handing out newspapers to passersby. The headline covered half the front page, screaming 'Shah is gone'. It showed a tired and defeated Shah, accompanied by his wife and three of their four children, saying goodbye to Prime Minister Bakhtiar.

Closer to the university, people had set up stalls selling books and journals that had previously been banned in Iran. Kamal stared hungrily at the titles. He bought Lenin's biography and another on the CIA's involvement in overthrowing Mossadeq in 1953.

He carried the books under his arm as he walked back to the office. He had been walking for two hours but didn't feel tired. He was buoyant. With each step, he dreamt of the Republic of Iran. He allowed himself, for the first time, to fantasise of the day he would finally get to vote for a democratic parliament.

When he reached his office he saw some of his staff celebrating in the foyer. As he walked past them he thought he heard one say, 'Your lot will be next.'

Mum sipped her tea slowly, occasionally blowing on it to cool it down further. She exchanged a look with Eshrat Mamman as the sound of a commotion began on the street.

'Stay here and watch your brother,' Mum said to me as she and Eshrat Mamman rose to investigate.

Just then Khaleh Soheyla, Mum's middle sister, burst into the room. She was breathless and her eyes danced with excitement.

'He's gone!' She said. 'The Shah's gone!' And she hugged Mum, squeezing her.

Mum, Behzad and I followed Soheyla to the street. The atmosphere was electric. Soheyla rushed across the street and came back with a bunch of flowers and some of our favourite sweets. She gave me the box of *zoolbiya*. 'Here, kids,' she opened the box for us, 'sweeten your mouths to celebrate this great moment.' Behzad and I were very excited to see my mum and my aunty so happy. We danced in front of my grandmother's front gate, too frightened to join the thick of the crowd. Mum and Soheyla handed out sweets to strangers and threw flowers into the crowd.

My grandmother never joined us. I found her crying in the corner of her room, holding the Shah's picture in her hands. Even though she was religious, Eshrat Mamman had a great fondness for the monarchy and mourned their loss for years to come.

The celebrations continued until late in the evening. That night we were thrilled to be allowed on the rooftop and enthusiastically shouted slogans into the cold night. 'Death to Shah. Death to America. Death to Carter. Allah-O-Akbar.'

We woke up excited. It was 1 February 1979, a bitterly cold day. A victorious Ayatollah Khomeini would soon be arriving in Tehran. Dad had bought Behzad a poster mounted on a stick of Khomeini and Behzad was waving it proudly around the house. Our school had remained closed all winter and he looked forward to getting out of the apartment. There was still a lot of unrest on the streets of Tehran. It seemed the different factions, which until now had been fighting side by side against the Shah, were now fighting one another for power.

We were no longer allowed to roam freely in the rubble behind our apartment. Many of our neighbours who had fled the country had released their dogs into the streets. The dogs fought with each other for scraps of food. The lucky ones were used as targets by the local youths with guns. Others died a slow death from hunger.

The radio confirmed that the Ayatollah's chartered Air France jetliner had left Paris and would be landing at Tehran's Mehrabad airport soon. The new revolutionary national television station showed footage of people lining the streets of Tehran chanting: 'Freedom. Imam Khomeini. Islam'. People were smiling into the camera. Men and women cried with joy. A mother carried a photo of her eighteen-year-old son who had died during the revolution.

A live telecast from the plane showed a French journalist interviewing the Ayatollah. 'Ayatollah Khomeini, what are your feelings going back to Iran after fourteen years in exile?'

Khomeini looked back at the reporter with eyes like coal, 'I feel nothing.' Mum paled. Her eyes, wide and bewildered. She walked up to the television and snapped it silent.

Mum refused to come with us that day. We drove towards the university. Dad parked the car and we walked as far as we could until the press of the crowd stopped us. The atmosphere was electric. People climbed over cars in the hope of getting a better view. Above us the trees cradled children and men in their branches.

Behzad tugged at Dad's shirt, 'Daddy, I can't see a thing.' Dad propped him onto his shoulders. Behzad beamed from where he sat, wrapping his small fingers proudly around his poster of Khomeini.

'Has Agha gone past yet?' Dad asked a man standing beside us with a transistor radio pressed to his ear.

'No, not yet. They should be here soon.' The man told us that the Ayatollah's plane had landed and he'd emerged victorious to greet the international media before being led to a blue Chevrolet Blazer.

In the distance we could hear the sound of beeping horns. *Beep. Beep. Bi-bi-beep.* The crowd pressed forward, stretching their necks to gain a better view. I stood on my tiptoes, holding on to Dad's arm for balance. The sound of the horns grew louder. A cheer rose from the people around us. Some began chanting slogans, punching their fists into the air.

The blue Chevrolet drove past slowly through the crowd, but all I saw were the people who had managed to climb on top of it. Behzad had raised his arms as far as he could over his head, waving his poster. Dad had to tighten his grip on Behzad's legs to stop him from falling.

The crowd cheered as Khomeini's entourage drove past, heading towards Behesht Zahra cemetery where the Ayatollah was to make his first speech. Later, back at home, we watched the Ayatollah standing amongst the graves of thousands who had died during the revolution against the Shah. He raised his fist in the air and declared the Bakhtiar regime was illegal.

'I will strike with my fists at the mouths of this government. From now on it is I who will name the government.'

The crowd rose to him with chants of *Allah-O-Akbar*.

On Friday morning, 9 February, Kamal woke early, lit a Rothmans and turned on his shortwave radio to the BBC.

'Shapoor Bakhtiar is still holding the post of Iran's Prime Minister,' the BBC announcer's voice filled the room. 'Despite this, within a week of arriving, the Ayatollah Khomeini has appointed his Islamic provisional government. The supporters of the Ayatollah have formed revolutionary committees around Tehran declaring themselves enforcers of law and order. Sources say street fighting has become fierce between the Ayatollah's supporters and the soldiers loyal to the Prime Minister Bakhtiar.

'This is the BBC World Service. In other news: in Britain 19 000 workers again went on strike at the Birmingham plant...'

Kamal stretched. He looked over to where Nina was still pretending to be asleep, her back to him and the radio. He traced his fingers along the lace of her nightgown.

Nina spoke, turning slowly to face him, 'I'm starting to think it was a mistake to support this revolution.'

'Anything will be better than living under a dictator,' Kamal replied. 'When the demon departs, the angels shall arrive.'

Nina sat up and reached for her dressing-gown. She climbed out of bed, pulled the gown over her shoulders and pulled the belt tight around her waist.

'It's very well to quote Hafez. But who's to say that this angel won't bring with it a bed of nails?'

On the same day — at two of Tehran's airforce spaces, Doshen Tappeh and Farhadabad — the Homafars who were responsible for the major technical upkeep of the airforce declared their allegiance to the Islamic revolution. Infuriated, the Javadans, the Shah's Imperial guards, attacked the bases. With the support of the armed revolutionaries the bases repelled the Javadans and other loyalists and in turn broke into the armoury, distributing weapons to revolutionaries and bystanders. The fighting continued all night. On the radio we could hear the announcements as one by one the police stations fell into the hands of the revolutionaries. As each police station surrendered new fear gripped us that we would have no protection against the fighting or looting.

From our roof we could see the red, angry skies above the burning city as the fierce fighting at the airforce base spilled into the surrounding neighbourhoods. The air grew thick with smoke. In the distance, the bursts of gunfire ripped through the night's edgeless blanket.

The next morning Nina was bent over her new gas heater. There was no electricity again and she was having some trouble making it work. She brought her candle closer to help her see better. It took her two goes before the heater flared into life. She straightened her back and stretched. Sirens were blaring in the distance. The sun was rising from the horizon like a red fireball. Columns of smoke rose to an apocalyptic sky. She stood motionless at the window.

'How did it all come to this?' She dropped her eyes, not wanting to see any more. She walked over to her samovar. The electric one sat useless next to her recently purchased oil-based one. She filled it with water and put two fresh eggs in the water. The merchant she had bought the eggs from had sensed that she was uncomfortable haggling, and had charged her a hefty price.

She replaced the samovar's lid and reached for her tea-leaves. A burst of gunfire startled her and the tin dropped from her hands, spilling the leaves all over the benchtop. She cursed silently as she collected the contents and placed them into a china teapot. Then she filled the pot with boiling water and placed it on top to brew.

Looking around for her packet of Rothmans, she thought about her promise to herself to quit smoking, but chose to ignore it. She pulled a cigarette out of the half-empty packet, lit it and drew deeply. It was getting harder to find Rothmans. She drew the smoke deep into her lungs. She closed her eyes as she exhaled, trying to block out the sirens and gunfire outside.

'Dear God, our protector, let there be peace,' she prayed, her lips hardly moving.

The smell of the brewed tea brought Nina back from her thoughts. She opened her eyes reluctantly and removed the teapot, half-filling her *estekan* with the strong brew and the rest with the boiling water from the samovar.

Kamal walked in, his expression grave. As he got closer, she noticed the red veins in the whites of his eyes.

'What's the matter, Kamal?' she said, her heart fluttering like a frightened bird.

'I was listening to the BBC. Bakhtiar has resigned after the airport showdown and has gone into hiding. The West is predicting a civil war in Iran.'

Nina went cold. In the background the sound of gunfire escalated. Kamal walked over to the window. The winter sky was heavy with smoke. He stared in the direction of the gunfire.

'It's not safe here. I want you and the children to go to London. At least until things settle down,' he continued staring out the window, avoiding her eyes.

'We won't go without you,' she said, without hesitation. Kamal hung his head, pressing his fingers to his temples.

'Nina, please. It will only be until things settle down,' he turned to face her and pleaded in a softer voice, 'think of the children.'

Nina stabbed the ashtray with her cigarette. 'I am thinking of the children,' she retorted. 'I don't want them to be fatherless. Why don't you come with us?'

'You know I can't leave work. The senior partners are still in Europe and they're not showing any signs of returning. And our staff are threatening to strike. The staff, who until a month ago were falling over themselves to please us, are now calling us bloodsuckers. If I leave now, I'll be letting down the whole firm. I can't do that.'

Nina squared her shoulders. 'Then we will all stay.' She poured another tea. 'We're a family and you are the head of this family.' She extended her arm, offering the tea to him. 'We won't go anywhere without you.'

Kamal moved closer to her. Her small frame only reached up to his chest. With one hand he cupped her face, turning it up to face him. 'Things could get much worse. We might not be able to get out later.'

'I will not leave without you.'

He dropped his hand. He took the tea from her and walked to the kitchen table where he dropped two sugar cubes into his glass. The sugar particles danced about the *estekan* like snowflakes in a storm until they dissolved.

The sirens outside punctured the silence between them. Nina watched Kamal stirring his tea for a while, then fetched the eggs out of the samovar. Leaving one to split between the children, she placed the other in an eggcup. Outside, the winter sun rose higher, spilling a thin light through the window. She placed the eggcup, a teaspoon and the salt shaker in front of Kamal.

'I'd sooner die than split up my family,' she said as she bent over to blow out the candle. He knew he could not convince her to do otherwise. She sat in the seat next to him, sipping her tea.

He reached over and kissed her pale lips.

'This is the sound of Radio Azadi. Last night Chief of Staff, General Ghara-Baghi, ordered all troops into their barracks. With the support of other generals, the army has declared itself neutral. The illegal government of Bakhtiar has now been decimated and our Imam Khomeini is victorious. Bakhtiar, who was appointed by the Shah to continue his satanic duties, has gone cowardly into hiding.'

'Jesus!' Kamal could hardly believe the national news. It was 12 February 1979.

'What does this all mean?' Nina asked, not sure if she wanted to know the answer.

'It means the generals have stopped a civil war from erupting.'

'Praise to God. That's great news.'

'Not exactly.'

'Doesn't this mean the fighting is over?' Nina asked, confused and a little frightened by Kamal's reaction.

'No . . . It means we're now at the mercy of trigger-happy revolutionaries.'

Eshrat Mamman

'I want to see Eshrat Mamman,' I insisted, my lips curled into a pout.

'Me too,' declared Behzad, stamping his feet. 'I've made her a drawing.'

Eshrat Mamman lived approximately an hour away, towards the southern part of Tehran. Her fridge was always filled with Kit Kats and Paddle Pops, which had become increasingly hard to find. She would scour the shops, tormenting shopkeepers and expertly haggling over the price.

Behzad and I would run in, heading straight for the kitchen where we knew she would be. She would sweep us into her open arms, stuffing our pockets with sweets and showering us with kisses. We had not seen her since the day the Shah left, and missed her as much as the sweets.

'Please, Mummy. Pleeeaaaase...' I persisted.

Mum looked unsure. She had too much on her mind to argue with us. 'Go ask your father,' she finally opted, passing on the decision to Dad. Secretly she would have liked to visit her mother, but the streets were still not safe.

We ran to our parents' room, forgetting to knock as we stormed in, pleading with our father. We raced back out of the bedroom.

'Daddy said we could go.' I beamed triumphantly at Mum as I reached for my coat.

'He did?' Mum raised her eyebrows in mock surprise.

I had put my coat on and was helping Behzad as he struggled into his. 'Really, Mummy. You should have known Daddy is a lot easier to convince than you.' I pulled my beanie over my ears and put on my boots.

'We'll be outside waiting till you come,' I called over my shoulder. 'Don't be long.' And I banged the door behind us, not looking back at Mum in case she tried to stop us.

In the car ride to Eshrat Mamman's house we were surprised by the increase in revolutionary guards on the streets with machine guns in hand. Blockades had been set up on every major road. But none of them seemed to pay much attention to the traffic that went past. Dad slowed down as we approached each blockade, ready to stop if he had to, but we were never stopped. It seemed the guards, most of whom looked to be in their late teens, were more interested in their new artillery. Occasionally one of them would fire his machine gun in to the air to the great cheer of the others. Behzad and I were happy to be going to see Eshrat Mamman. We bounced on our seats talking excitedly about seeing her. Mum and Dad were quieter. Mum's shoulders would tense every time we came close to a road block. She flinched at the sound of guns firing. Occasionally she pressed the middle of her forehead as if releasing a sharp pain. I noticed her fingers trembled slightly when she did that. Next to her, Dad gripped the wheel with both hands, leaning into it. His head moved from side to side, taking in the destruction around him. I noticed a strain around his eyes that reminded me of the day at the beach when we heard about the demonstrations in Tehran's streets.

We turned left into Pahlavi Street. Shells of burned cars were left discarded on the side of the streets. There were slogans painted on walls and rubbish choked the gutters. The streets were deserted.

Dad looked into his rearview mirror. 'Dear God!' He turned and looked over his shoulder as if he didn't trust the reflection. 'There's a tank behind us!'

We all turned in our seats to look. Behind us was a full-size army tank. The door to the cabin was open and a revolutionary guard stood halfway out of it. He had his rifle held over his head with both hands as a sign of victory. There were four other revolutionaries in army greens sitting on the body of the tank. Smiling behind their beards, they raised their rifles proudly into the air. Their right hands, curled into tight fists, punched the air in unison. With each raised fist they chanted: 'Death to America. Death to America.'

Behzad, excited by what he saw, joined their chorus. 'Death to America,' his small fist imitating the guards.

Mum and Dad shared a look but said nothing.

Once we got to Eshrat Mamman's house, Behzad and I raced each other through the front garden, past the fifty-year-old cherry tree and up the stairs to her front door where she was waiting for us with outstretched arms. I adored my grandmother with an intensity which I reserved for her alone.

'My darlings. How my heart has ached from being separated from you.' She squeezed us into her chest then straightened up and berated my parents for not bringing us to her sooner. Mum simply nodded as she walked through the front door. She had learned from an early age not to argue with her mother.

Behzad tugged at Eshrat Mamman's skirt, 'I've made a drawing for you.' He reached into his parka and pulled out a folded piece of white paper. He unfolded it and handed it to her, all the while beaming with pride.

'Thank you, my angel,' she beamed back, admiring Behzad's dark eyes and lashes. 'You and your sister run along to the kitchen. I've got something special for you on the bench.'

Eshrat Mamman followed the children with her eyes, her lips moving rapidly, whispering a prayer under her breath. She finished the prayer with a *salavat,* her eyes and palms heaven bound. She made a mental note to burn some *esfand* later to keep away the evil eye. Only then did she look down at the picture Behzad had drawn. Colour drained from her face. She blinked to regain focus.

'Nina!' she said with a tight voice and squeezed her daughter's arm as she handed her the drawing. 'Have you seen this?'

Nina's face twisted with grief.

The picture was of a battle. Stick figures with rifles fired their guns at one another. Corpses lay in pools of blood, some with their limbs missing. In the middle of the battle scene, Behzad had drawn several explosions with thick smoke rising from them.

Nina's face was blurred by the tears she fought hard to hold back. 'That's all he seems to be drawing these days. That's not all. He's been having nightmares, waking up crying. Some nights when I go to check on him, I find him rocking in his bed.' She inhaled short bursts of air through her nose, trying to regain her composure. Failing, she let go. She wiped her face with the back of her hand.

Eshrat Mamman stroked her daughter's back with sad affection. Nina seemed relieved that she could finally speak openly. 'I talked to a child psychologist. She told me he's traumatised. Can you believe it! My-seven-year-old is trauma-tised.' Nina turned to look at her, but Mamman had lost her strength. Mamman's eyes stung and her vision blurred. She blinked rapidly a few times but was unable to hold back the single tear that traced the side of her face, following the fine creases etched with age.

'She said it's normal for children in war zones to draw these pictures,' Nina continued, stabbing the drawing with her index finger. 'It's an outlet for them.' She snorted and looked down at her hands, unfolding the picture with trembling fingers.

'This is all my fault. I've done this to my child. And what's worse is that their school is not reopening. They have to go to public schools. God only knows how Behzad's going to handle it there.' Her eyes moved skyward as if sending a plea to a higher being. Tears rolled down her face, pausing on her chin like raindrops on gutters, before falling onto the folded drawing.

We finished our lunch and Eshrat Mamman and Mum were in the kitchen preparing tea. Throughout the lunch they had sat close with their heads together. When I had followed them to the kitchen with the dirty dishes, I found them hugging as if holding on to one another for support.

I was sent back with a tray, carrying the *estekans* and a bowl of sugar lumps. In the living room Dad was sitting on the floor with his head resting against the wall. He had his eyes shut. Behzad was playing soldiers with his action man. He would raise the action man's hand above its head while calling out, 'Death to America.' Action man would then open fire with his plastic rifle, killing all.

Just as Mum walked in, carrying the tea and dates, the front doorbell buzzed. Eshrat Mamman picked up the intercom. 'Yes...Mahmood, is that you? Come on in, son.'

A few minutes later Mahmood walked in carrying a large army bag. Mahmood is married to Mum's younger sister Soheyla. Of average height and slim, he had thick black curly hair and a bushy moustache, in line with the revolutionary style. His eyes, behind his black-rimmed glasses, were animated.

'*Salaam*,' he said respectfully, greeting the elders before kissing our foreheads, smelling of the cheap cigarettes he smoked. He then turned to Dad who was blinking the sleep out of his eyes.

'Agha Kamal. Could I see you for a minute?' Dad nodded reluctantly and followed Mahmood and his army bag out of the room.

Upstairs in one of the guestrooms, Mahmood placed the bag on a bed. With his back to Kamal he unzipped the bag then stepped aside so Kamal could take a look. Kamal stepped forward, studying the curious expression on Mahmood's face.

'What's this all about, Mahmood? What are you carrying in that bag?'

'Why don't you take a look for yourself?' Mahmood replied excitedly, all the time watching the door over his shoulder. Kamal reached inside the bag and pulled out an old blanket. Beneath it there were five G3 rifles.

'*Allah-O-Akbar!* Have you gone mad?' He lowered his voice so it wouldn't be carried downstairs. 'What the hell are you doing with these?'

Mahmood picked one up and ran his fingers along the rifle's streamlined contour. 'Do you know what they are?' He aimed the rifle at an imaginary target.

Kamal ripped the rifle out of Mahmood's hands and threw it back on the bed with disgust. 'Of course I do. I spent two years in the army as a conscript. Where did you get these from anyway?'

Mahmood shrugged his shoulders. 'One of my friends was at the barracks last night when they were raided. He just gave them to me.'

Kamal felt his anger rising. 'Why did you bring them here?'

'Because I asked him to,' a deep voice answered from the doorway, surprising both men. Ghasem Sadraii's large frame filled the doorway. He wore a thick woollen cardigan stretched over his large stomach, and pleated pyjama pants. His face was clean-shaven and cologned. He walked heavily towards his sons-in-law.

'Son...' he paused, gathering his thoughts. When he spoke again his words were measured. 'I am the man of the house. As you know, we are living in uncertain times. The Shah's gone, and with him the old regime. To many I represent the old regime.'

Kamal looked at his father-in-law. He'd been a colonel in the Shah's police force for many years. Everyday there were rumours about generals and officials being arrested or executed.

'I need to protect my family at all cost,' the colonel said.

Kamal clenched his hands to stop them from shaking. 'I respect your concern. But I can assure you,' pointing to the rifles with trembling fingers, 'this is not the way.'

'This is the only way!' Colonel Sadraii bellowed.

'No. No, it's not.' Kamal turned away from the two men. He ran a hand through his hair. He stared out the window to the three-metre wall which separated the house from the street.

'Are you going to kill every man that jumps over that?' Kamal pointed at the wall. Dropping his arm, he turned and faced his father-in-law, 'Because if they come, they won't be in ones and twos.'

Colonel Sadraii shifted his weight as if trying to release a tension in his legs. He walked towards the bed and leaned heavily on the mattress as he lowered himself down. He looked at the rifles. A deep crease formed between his brows. He stared at the weapons for a long time.

Kamal and Mahmood stood patiently, waiting for him to speak again. Colonel Sadraii rubbed his smooth face with his thick fingers. He looked at his sons-in-law with strained eyes.

'Mahmood,' he finally said, 'take these rifles out of my house.'

Mahmood opened his mouth as if to object, but thought better of it. He hastily rewrapped the rifles in the old blanket and placed them back in the army bag. He mumbled a goodbye and walked quickly out of the room. Colonel Sadraii stretched on the bed with his eyes fixed at a spot on the ceiling. Kamal placed a hand on the old man's shoulder. 'I think you made the right decision, Colonel.'

'God be willing, we shall all survive this madness,' the colonel said in a tight voice. He rolled uneasily onto his side, turning his back to Kamal.

By the time we arrived home the streets were dark. Mum and Dad barely spoke throughout the trip. Behzad had fallen asleep holding his action man close to his chest. His body rocked gently.

It was dark inside the apartment stairwell. Mamman was upstairs at Shahin's place. By the time we parked the car Mamman and Shapoor were waiting for us at the stairs in front of our apartment with a gaslight that flickered orange on the walls and steps. We made our way carefully up the stairs, while Dad walked behind us with Behzad in his arms.

Inside our apartment, Shapoor pulled Dad aside. 'There's going to be a neighbourhood meeting.'

Dad passed Behzad to Mum and turned to face Shapoor.
'What for?'

'I'm not sure. Everyone's been really nervous since the
barracks fell into the hands of the revolutionaries...things
seem to have taken a new turn.'

'What time's the meeting?'

'Seven-thirty at Haji's house across the street.'

Haji greeted each man at the door of his modest apartment.
He stood a little stooped, as if weighed down by age and worry,
and leaned heavily on his cane when he walked.

The neighbourhood men were led into Haji's best room,
which was lit with candles and decorated with heavy baroque
furniture and a large Persian carpet. Kamal recognised almost
all of the twenty or so men who had come and nodded his
head in greeting to them. Most were around his age, family
men with young kids. There were a couple of older men, well
into their sixties with balding temples and sagging bellies. They
sat at the head of the room, close to Haji, in deference to
their age. Haji's wife offered tea to the men before leaving
soundlessly, closing the French doors behind her. Haji sat at
the head of the room. He pulled his worry beads out of his
pocket and started rolling them between his fingers.

'*Bisme-Allah-Rahmanel-Rahim.* I wish to firstly thank all you
friends for giving up your evening to join us in our humble
home,' he paused, not wishing to rush his words.

'Since last night our streets have been left at the mercy of
the revolutionaries. As you have no doubt heard, the army has
withdrawn its support for Bakhtiar. There are no longer any

armed forces which can protect our homes and our families from the looters.'

Kamal looked around the room. Most of the men were nodding. All wore worried expressions, made even graver by the shadows formed by the candlelight.

'So,' Haji continued, 'I propose we form a neighbourhood watch.' He paused in case anyone objected to his proposal. No one did. 'We'll start tonight and rotate the men every four hours until daybreak. Which one of you gentlemen has been in the army?' Kamal raised his hand along with two others. The rest stared at the floor, avoiding their neighbours' eyes.

Haji scanned the room. 'It seems there are only three amongst us,' he raised and dropped his shoulders with a sigh and a small shake of the head. 'If you agree, gentlemen, due to your familiarity with the armoury, you will be the group leaders.'

After the meeting, standing on the roof in the bitter cold night, Kamal cursed himself for raising his hand. As one of the first watchmen, Haji had supplied him with a metal dish, a metal serving spoon and a whistle. Those on watch were supposed to frighten away the mobs by banging the spoon against the dish while blowing their whistle. The other neighbourhood men were then meant to pour out of their warm beds with their sticks and shovels to defend their homes and families against the armed looters.

Kamal chuckled and shook his head. It's been a crazy day, he thought, as he shone the torch on his watch: 11.55 pm.

'Good. Only five more minutes.' He rubbed his hands together. His leather driving gloves did little to warm them.

He pulled the collar of his parka over his ears. The past four hours had passed peacefully and quietly. There had hardly been any gunfire. From where he stood he could see over the blackened city illuminated only by the light of the moon. The stars were still hidden behind a blanket of heavy clouds.

A few minutes later Kamal crawled into bed, wrapping himself around Nina's warm body. She flinched at the touch of his cold skin against hers.

'How was it?' she asked, her voice heavy with sleep.

'It was freezing. Thankfully though, nothing happened.' He pressed closer against her. 'I overheard one of our neighbours say that Khomeini went on air, declaring it *haram*, a forbidden act, to steal another brother's property.'

Like many others in neighbourhoods around Tehran they spent a restless night, their senses alert to sounds coming from the street.

Komiteh

Nina entered the lift, pulled out the letter from her handbag and opened it. It was from the Komiteh of Conservation of the Revolution requesting her to report to them on the sixth floor in the Ministry of Health building. The lifts opened to a foyer she had rarely visited in all her years at the ministry. A man with an angular face and a bushy moustache sat behind a desk, talking rapidly into a phone. A handwritten sign above him told Nina she was at the right place.

The Komiteh were committees organised around neighbourhood mosques and within student and workers groups. Headed mainly by mullahs and vigilantes, they had originally formed the front-line of anti-Shah demonstrations and strikes. The majority were overwhelmingly Islamist and viewed themselves as the guardians of the revolution. In 1979, the Komiteh had established themselves as a rival authority to the police and conducted arbitrary arrests and raids on private homes confiscating liquor, Western music or anything else that might be offensive to their Islamic sensitivities.

Nina waited for the man to finish his phone call before introducing herself.

'Wait over at the bench, sister. They will come and get you.'

Nina sat on the hard wooden bench staring at the picture of Khomeini on the wall. Once in a while men with beards or women in chador walked past in rapid steps.

Before the revolution she had worked at the Ministry of Health under Dr Aram for five years as director of nurses. Her gentle hands and natural rapport with babies made her an ideal midwife. Over the years luck and determination had taken her to the top of her profession, away from the hospital floor and into administration. She thought about her boss, Dr Aram. He had been arrested in the 1978 revolution and jailed by the Shah to demonstrate that even officials in high government posts were not exempt from reform. On the night the barracks were raided, the political prisoners were freed. Some, like Dr Aram, were released accidentally. Once they realised their mistake the revolutionary guards had tried to rearrest Dr Aram, but he had disappeared. One of the rumours circulating the Ministry of Health was that Dr Aram had escaped to Turkey with his family, disguised as a woman. Nina smiled to herself imagining her boss escaping by night under the veil of a chador, wrapped head to toe in the black Islamic garb.

Nina shifted in her seat. In the past hour no one had spoken or even looked at her. There were now others who were also waiting along the corridor. The air was hot and stale and her throat felt dry.

Two men approached the desk and spoke briefly with the man sitting behind it.

'Dastyari,' the man at the desk called.

Nina stood a little unsteady on her legs. The two men turned and looked at her. She did not recognise them as they walked towards her with heavy steps that drummed against the concrete floor. Nina took an involuntary step backwards as the men reached her. They were both unshaven and smelt of cheap cigarettes.

'Turn around,' one of them said in a gravelly voice.

'What for?' Nina asked, her throat tightening.

One of them grabbed her shoulder and spun her hard on her heels. Surprised by the force of the turn, Nina lost her footing and nearly fell. Before she could get her bearings back, she was pulled upright by her arms. Then, her vision went black.

Fear like a tidal wave rose from her stomach, making her knees go weak. A sharp pain pressed at the back of her eyes as a blindfold was tied into a tight knot behind her.

'Where are you taking me?' she said, trying hard to control the shaking in her voice.

Each man grabbed one of her arms and pushed her forward between them.

Nina tried to resist. 'Where are you taking me?' she asked again and then, almost in a pleading voice, 'Please, I have done nothing wrong.'

'Shut up,' the gravelly voice said. 'The time when you *Savaki* stooges could order us about is over.'

They turned a corner and she was ordered to stop. She heard the click of a door and the croak of its hinges reluctantly opening. She could hear muffled voices of people talking on the other side of the door but they stopped when it opened. She felt unsteady and dizzy as she was led to a chair. The air around her was thick with cigarette smoke and the sweat of people kept too long together in a confined space. She was asked to remove her blindfold. She blinked several times before her eyes adjusted. When she did, fear like a fist lodged itself in her chest, winding her. She sat at the end of a conference table and at the other end four people, their identities masked behind veils like dark ghosts, sat in an arc.

She had seen similar images on television, where the shrouded figures would denounce people as the enemies of the revolution. Their voices would rise in a high pitch as they announced to the cameras that justice would finally be served. The accused would stand motionless, blindfolded with hands tied behind their back. Underneath their blindfolds were patches of discoloured skin. Their accusers would point to them and call them a 'thorn' in the side of the Iranian people before announcing their execution at dawn.

The man with the gravelly voice sat on a chair between Nina and the four at the other end of the table.

'*Bisme-Allah-Rahmanel-Rahim*,' he began. 'You are being accused, sister,' he said reading from the piece of paper before him, 'of treachery towards the Iranian people.'

Nina's breath left her.

'By whom?'

'Quiet!' he snapped. 'There are several charges against you from your colleagues.'

Her throat felt squeezed, constricted. She closed her eyes murmuring '*Ya Ali*' over and over.

The man slapped the table hard. Nina's eyes snapped open.

'What do you say to the charges of being a SAVAK spy?' He spat the words at her.

She looked at the four at the other end of the table. 'What proof do you have? What have I done for you to accuse me of being a spy?'

Nina began shivering despite the acrid heat of the room. She needed a drink of water and she pulled at the knot of her scarf.

The four at the end wrote notes on pieces of paper which they handed to the man. He read each note with great interest.

'It seems clear to me, sister, that you have a lot to answer for.'

After three hours they finally let her go. She was again blindfolded before leaving the room.

'We know where you live,' the gravelly voice had hissed into her ear. 'The days of *Tagootis* like yourself parading like peacocks are over. The Islamic Republic is going to teach you a lesson you will never forget.'

Outside the sky had turned the colour of lead. Nina's legs shook as she walked to her car. She needed a cigarette but had not dared to stop to find one in her handbag. Once inside the car she locked her door and tried to slow down her breath. She could not believe they had accused her of being Dr Aram's mistress and supplying women to him and his colleagues. Then there were the usual accusations of being a SAVAK agent. Finally she had received a *hokm* to be demoted from her position from the Ministry of Health, and placed as the matron of Darbar hospital, a small hospital that had served the palace staff before the revolution and since then had become insignificant. She did not want the position. She feared her days would be spent defending herself against false accusations and having her authority challenged by subordinates.

She reached into her handbag for her cigarettes. Her fingers shook as she fumbled with her lighter but before she could light it she was overcome with nausea. She unlocked her door and heaved. Each wave of nausea wrenched her stomach and shook her small frame. By the time she was heaving dry bitter bile a cold damp covered her skin. She continued to heave, wanting to rid herself of each humiliation and hateful accusation hurled at her.

End of a dream

Nina sat at the kitchen table waiting for Kamal to finish his breakfast. They were both dressed in jeans and jumpers. She played absentmindedly with the tassels on her woollen scarf. This was the first demonstration they were attending since the return of the Ayatollah.

Iran was going to have a referendum in March. Khomeini had handpicked Prime Minister Bazargan for his new Provisional Revolutionary Government. Like his predecessor, Bazargan was Western-educated and believed in parliamentary democracy, basic freedoms and respect for the individuals. He had spent many years in the Shah's prisons. He was also a deeply religious man and popular among Iran's educated middle class. He argued that the electorate should be given a choice between a secular or religious form of government. The Ayatollah had rejected the idea, insisting on an Islamic constitution. The referendum was to decide whether Iran should become 'The

Islamic Republic' or not. Kamal talked excitedly about voting for the first time between mouthfuls of cornflakes. Today's demonstrations were in support of the 'no' vote, with a view to Iran becoming 'The Democratic Republic of Iran' instead.

Nina's eyes and mind wandered outside, past the frosted window to the majestic snowcapped Alborz Mountains that rose out of the horizon.

After her visit to the Komiteh she had refused to accept her demotion to matron of Darbar hospital. She had waited for hours to plead her case with a colleague who still held a high position.

'You've been labelled with Aram's stamp,' his voice echoed in her head. 'No one wants to work with you.' He told her to lay low for six months. She could even stay at her position and salary, but her duties would be reduced to menial tasks. After six months he would try and find her a better job. As the news spread of her demotion, more and more of her colleagues distanced themselves. She didn't blame them. The same fear that SAVAK had ruled with before now echoed in the corridors of the Komiteh.

She had tried to speak to Kamal about it but his answer was always the same. 'Of course there are going to be changes. It's a revolution. But things will settle down, you'll see. The important issue here is that the old regime is dead. We now have a real chance to live in a democratic society.' But these days his words held less conviction. Recently she also noticed a strain in his voice that had not been there a few months ago.

—◊—

The demonstrators met at the gates of Tehran University. By 10 am there was already a crowd of a few thousand gathering in support of a Democratic Republic of Iran. The people looked different to those in previous demonstrations. The men were clean-shaven. Most of the women wore make-up and traces of perfume. Nina, along with many others, was not wearing a hejab. Both the men and women were dressed casually in European labels. The mood was festive and Kamal and Nina felt buoyant with the atmosphere. The air was crisp and the sun shone through the hazy sky, slowly melting the ice into a brown slush.

The procession began soon after. 'Peace...Freedom... Democratic Iran!' were the cries heard from the crowd. Kamal squeezed Nina's hand. People were gathering in numbers, their voices more confident.

In the distance there was a roar of speeding trucks. At first it was no more than a faint sound amongst the traffic from the surrounding streets. But the sound of the heavy wheels crunching on gravel became louder and several trucks could be seen heading towards the demonstrators. Some of the crowd slowed down, curious about the trucks, but most of them pressed forward, shouting louder to be heard. The trucks forced their way into the middle of the group, breaking their unity, and men jumped out of the back of the trucks drowning out the voices of the crowd with loudspeaker slogans of their own.

'Death to America. Death to Carter.'

'Allah-O-Akbar. Khomeini Rahbar.'

'The only republic is the Islamic Republic.'

The demonstrators still pressed forward. A few scuffles broke out. Nina pressed her hand tighter into Kamal's. People were pushing from behind and trucks blocked the front.

'Nina, this is getting ugly,' Kamal shouted over the roar of the loudspeakers. 'Let's get out of here.' She nodded. Colour had drained from her face. Kamal looked about him for a way out through the crowd. They heard screams coming from the direction of the trucks. Kamal looked up and saw the men on the trucks throwing large rocks at people in the crowd.

People were yelling. Kamal tightened his grip on Nina's hand as he pressed through. Someone screamed next to him. He turned to look at a man holding his head, blood streaming through his fingers as his companion pressed him to his chest.

'Help us, please. My friend's hurt. Brother, please help,' the man pleaded to people around him. No one listened. No one stopped. Fear, like bile, rose through Kamal's throat. People pushed from all direction. He felt Nina's hand slipping through his.

'Nina, hold on!' he shouted and turned to pull her towards him. Her face and jacket were sprayed with blood. She was staring at the injured man with shock. Two men had stopped to help. They were lifting the almost-unconscious man.

'Nina, are you hurt?' Kamal asked, pulling her into his arms. Nina shook her head. 'It's not my blood,' she said.

'Nina, no matter what happens, do not let go of my hand.'

The crowd pressed against them, restricting their oxygen. A sea of noise surrounded them. Kamal grabbed hold of Nina's hand, squeezing her fingers. She looked nauseous and shut her eyes to the chaos around her.

Kamal pushed his way towards the side streets, away from the men on the trucks and their loudspeakers. Frightened faces surrounded them, pressing and pushing one another, looking for a way out. Nina's small hand felt fragile in his. She had trouble keeping up with him. Suddenly she tripped and fell, breaking their grip.

'Ninaaaaa,' Kamal dived after her, pushing people out of his way. He groped desperately around people to find her arm. The crowd kept getting in between them. He felt her hands grabbing weakly onto his arm. He took her arm and braced himself as he pulled. A few times he nearly lost his own balance, he was losing his grip on her again. His heart pounded in his chest.

'Don't let go of my hand!' His voice was lost in the noise around them. Suddenly he felt her rise to her feet. A stranger had helped lift her up. Her face and hair were streaked with mud and blood. There was fear and confusion in her eyes.

Kamal turned to thank the man but he was already gone, lost in the crowd. Kamal looked about him. The crowd was thinning in an area to their left. He pointed to show Nina which way they had to go. He wrapped an arm tightly around her waist, and with his free arm pushed their way towards the clearing.

They followed a group of people running into the surrounding alleyway, not knowing where they were heading. In the scuffle, Kamal had lost a shoe and hobbled unsteadily on the muddy streets. Behind them they could hear the fighting. And amongst the confusion and the screams they could still make out the sound of the loudspeakers.

'The only republic is the Islamic Republic.'

—∿∿—

There were long queues in front of the polling stations on 30 March 1979. Kamal, excited by the prospect of voting for the first time, had lined up for hours. His heart felt like a caged bird. He kept patting his chest pocket where he kept his identity card. This was the first time it was going to be stamped for voting. He pulled it out and looked through it. It was already filled with ration stamps for rice, sugar, eggs and fuel.

A truck went past with a man shouting into a loudspeaker, 'Vote YES for the Islamic Republic.'

Kamal handed his card over to the polling official, who promptly stamped it and handed it back to him with a voting form. He read the form carefully, placing a clear tick in the box for the 'no' vote. The events of the previous few weeks — the escalation in fighting between factions, the closing down of many free press and the attacks during demonstrations — had not dampened his dreams of living in a democratically governed country.

That evening, the new revolutionary television station which had replaced the Shah's national television service proudly reported that there was a ninety per cent turnout with an overwhelming majority voting 'yes' for an Islamic Republic. Kamal switched off the television and sat staring at the black screen.

Black market

'Daddy, where are we going?'

We had been driving for almost an hour. It was May 1979 and we were in the south of Tehran. The roads were packed with cars, motorbikes and bicycles. Dad scanned the pavements, oblivious to the vehicles tooting at him for driving too slowly. Next to him was an empty packet of Rothmans. He absent-mindedly picked it up, looked through the small opening at the top, and frowned as he shook the packet. Disappointed, he crumpled the packet and threw it on the passenger seat.

'Daddy?'

'Shush! Keep your eyes open. Tell me if you see any street vendors.'

A woman in a black chador ran in front of our car towards the other side of the road, fearlessly dragging a young child behind her. Dad swore under his breath as he slammed on the brakes. He wiped away the small beads of sweat gathered below his hairline and gently pressed down on the accelerator. My father had learned to drive in England and still had trouble accepting the unwritten laws of Tehran's traffic.

He braked suddenly again. From the backseat I had to extend my arms to stop from slamming into the back of the driver's seat. Dad double-parked the car, switched off the engine and took out the key.

'Stay in the car and keep the doors locked. I'll be back soon,' he said with his eyes fixed on a group of people huddled on the footpath. He walked quickly towards them. At the centre of the group stood a short stocky man with a bushy moustache. Dad said something to him and the man shook his head. He offered Dad two packs of KitKat, but Dad waved the chocolates away and ran back to our car.

'Why didn't you buy them?' I asked, disappointed.

He looked at me as if surprised to find me in the backseat. 'Sorry.'

He pushed his way back into the traffic. We had not driven far when we saw a car stopping. The driver got out of the vehicle and walked to its rear. He looked about him before opening the boot. Dad slowed down. He narrowed his eyes until they were no more than slits. He scratched above his upper lip where he was growing a moustache in the new revolutionary style.

We watched the man reach inside the trunk and pull out a large green suitcase that had faded with age. He grabbed the handle with both hands and dragged it towards a willow tree. From there he would be slightly hidden while having a perfect view of the entire street.

A car in front of us pulled out from the curb and Dad quickly took its place. 'I won't be long,' he said over his shoulder. I locked the doors and sat close to the window, following Dad with my eyes.

'Brother, what are you selling?' Kamal asked, using the new term for addressing other men. The man had his back to the street and had not heard Kamal approaching. He turned, startled, but when he saw it was not the revolutionary guards he relaxed a little.

'I'm not selling anything,' the man rebuffed.

Kamal ignored his answer. 'I want cigarettes.'

'Don't have any...come back tomorrow.'

'I want a box of Rothmans...today,' Kamal said, moving closer to the man.

'I told you to come back tomorrow,' the man said, turning away from him.

'Listen here.' Grabbing the man's arm, Kamal leaned forward till his face was only inches away. He could smell a mixture of garlic and cigarettes on the man's breath. 'I'm not coming back. I need...I *want* these cigarettes today. If you don't sell them to me I'll find someone else.'

The man nodded and smiled reassuringly, revealing stained teeth. He raised his palms in a pacifying manner. 'Brother, there is no need for you to get angry. I might have something in my case to suit your needs.'

The man opened the suitcase slightly, careful not to reveal the contents to Kamal. 'Now let me see...I have some chocolates...all the way from America...'

'Cigarettes!' Kamal said in a raised voice and then, as if realising his mistake, looked about him and added in a lower voice, 'I want cigarettes.'

'Okay, brother,' the man said, raising his palms and looking about to see if they'd been heard.

'Well, let's see — how about a box of Marlboros?'

'Stop wasting my time. I said I want Rothmans.'

'Rothmans are becoming as rare as the royal blood.'

'I'll pay.'

'You have very expensive taste.' The man's lips spread into a smile but his eyes remained cold.

'How much?'

The man reached inside his case and pulled out two cartons of Rothmans. Kamal figured the two cartons would last them three weeks.

'Do you have any more?' he asked quickly.

The man snorted. 'Where do you think this is? America? Do you know what I had to do to get these?' He cradled the cartons in the crook of his arm.

'Okay, okay. How much?' Kamal reached inside his coat jacket for his wallet.

Dad walked back to the car. There was something large tucked under his jacket. His faced beamed like a child's at a birthday party. He climbed into the car and threw a couple of Kit Kats on my lap.

'Make sure you keep one for your brother,' he said, and winked at me.

The colonel

The shrill ringing of the phone jolted Nina. She was enjoying one of those rare moments when there were no children or Kamal to interrupt her enjoyment of silence. At first she thought of ignoring it, then thought better of it. She picked up the receiver and pressed it against her ear.

'Allo?'

'Nina?' It was Jalal. 'I need to speak to Kamal.'

Nina sensed the disturbance in Jalal's voice. 'What's happened?'

Jalal hesitated. 'I think it's best if I speak to Kamal first.'

A chill like ice water ran down her. 'Are Helen and the kids all right?'

'Yes, they are fine. Helen sends her greetings.'

'Kiss them from me,' she said. 'Wait. I'll get Kamal for you.'

Nina fetched Kamal from the garage, where he and the other men from the household were putting up shelves in the storage room. Ration coupons were required for everything and there were long queues, but most things could be found on the black market. All extra food items were now kept in the household storage room, which was locked with a padlock. Despite the shortages, there was enough food in there to feed the families for months.

Kamal grabbed the phone with wood-dust-covered hands. Nina stood close to him, her eyes never leaving his face. As he listened, Kamal's fingers tightened around the receiver. He shot Nina a look. Nina's pulse quickened high in her throat. He remained mainly silent throughout the call, rubbing his temples as he let out a heavy breath through his nose. Nina watched him hang up and then he continued to stare at the receiver. She wrapped her arms around her body, bracing herself against bad news.

'What's happened?'

Kamal shook his head. 'It's your father.'

'What about my father?'

'He's been arrested.'

Since Khomeini's arrival the chaos and uncertainty in Iran had continued. There had been many killings between Khomeini's guards, the Mojahedin, the communist Tudeh and the Fadayeen. All of whom, until recently, had fought together against the Shah. There had been regular executions since March. A new fear was spreading in people's hearts. There were frequent reports of house raids and of men, women, and even children, being sent before the firing squads.

Colonel Sadraii sat in the backseat of the Komiteh car. His large frame was squeezed between two youths with unshaven faces and green armbands. The windows had been rolled up and the car reeked of human sweat and fear. The vinyl upholstery squeaked whenever anyone moved in their seat.

The guards sat silently with their machine guns between their knees and their eyes fixed straight ahead. The colonel sat upright, his eyes following the road. They were driving him to the heart of southern Tehran.

In his head he carried the image of his wife sitting on the front steps of their veranda, hitting herself over the head with both hands and crying. He had always imagined they would come at night, but they had come in the morning. They had climbed onto their roof from the adjoining house. There were seven of them in total, all with machine guns. They had dragged him out of his room where he was reading his paper. He had not tried to resist. His wife had pleaded with them.

'Have mercy. He's an old man,' she had repeated over and over to no avail.

Colonel Sadraii felt large beads of sweat gather on his forehead. 'Where are you taking me?' he asked.

One of the guards ran his eyes over him but said nothing.

The Komiteh was set up next to a mosque, in a room the size of a classroom. The white-washed walls were lit by a naked light bulb which hung from the ceiling. A framed poster of Khomeini stared down from the wall.

Chairs were scattered along the wall where men and women sat segregated with worried expressions and hung heads. There were men with open-necked shirts and gold chains. The colonel guessed they were probably bazaar merchants who had been caught selling blackmarket goods. Others were younger men, most likely students being accused of communism. Some sat with ashen expressions, while others sat straight with their heads resting on the wall behind them and a defiant look in their eyes.

On the other side of the room in the women's section there were mainly well-dressed young women. They were no different from his younger daughter, Gita, who was only seventeen, he thought sadly. Some were crying, blowing their noses in their tissues. Others stared blankly at a spot on the floor. At the head of the room, on a raised platform, a mullah sat behind a desk covered with paperwork and a phone. He wore a white turban and heavy robes that draped to the floor. Next to him sat a thin man in a crumpled brown suit without a necktie. He sat very straight and still, his hands folded neatly over his lap. One of the guards walked up and whispered in his ear, pointing to the colonel as he handed him a folder. The thin man followed the guard's finger to where the colonel was sitting. He took the folder in his spidery fingers and opened it. After a few minutes he closed the folder and placed it on top of a stack of others.

The mullah, oblivious to the other two men, played with his bushy beard and peered over his round-rimmed glasses as he listened to the explanation of a woman being accused of wearing make-up in the street. He listened patiently, nodding his understanding. When she was finished, he wrote out a heavy fine and a caution that next time she disobeyed the Islamic laws she would be punished severely. He then dismissed her with a wave of his hand.

The man sitting next to the mullah handed him the colonel's folder and nodded to the guard standing behind the colonel. The guard tapped the colonel on the shoulder. 'You're next.'

The colonel felt his knees go weak. His frame sagged heavily, making it harder to walk. The guard pressed the butt of his gun into the small of the colonel's fleshy back and pushed him forward. Sadraii stood where the woman had been while the mullah's eyes scanned the contents of the folder, resting at a point on top of the page. His eyes narrowed. Slowly, the mullah lowered the folder to get a better look at the man before him.

'Colonel Ghasem Sadraii?'

'Yes.' The colonel's tongue felt swollen and stuck.

'Speak louder so Agha can hear you,' the guard behind him ordered.

'Yes, Agha.' Sadraii lifted his head so the sound would carry better.

'Did you have a post in Bandar Abbas before coming to Tehran?'

'Yes, Agha.'

The mullah clapped his hands and rose to his feet, surprising everyone. He walked towards the colonel with outstretched arms. Sadraii took a step back into the guard standing behind him, but the mullah embraced him and kissed his cheeks. The thin man also stood up and looked to the guard for an explanation. The guard shrugged his shoulders and shook his head.

'This is a great man!' the mullah announced to all that were present in the room. 'Twenty years ago when that devil worshipping Shah exiled those of us who spoke against him to Bandar Abbas on the Persian Gulf, this man here showed us kindness instead of torment.'

Sadraii started to shake as relief washed over him. The mullah put his arm around him and the colonel, finally overcome, placed his head in the crook of the mullah's neck and sobbed.

Colonel Sadraii left the Komiteh with a letter from the mullah in his breast pocket. He patted his chest to make sure the letter was real. Outside, Jalal was waiting for him in a police car. He helped the exhausted colonel into the frontseat. Once inside the car, Sadraii opened the letter again. He had already read it half a dozen times. The mullah, in his own hand, had written that the colonel was a personal friend of his and not to be harassed or arrested under any circumstances.

Kamal sat behind his desk with one elbow on the arm of his leather chair, supporting his head in his hand. A letter sat in front of him.

The letterhead read 'The Islamic Ministry of Finance'. It was one of many the accountancy firm had received in the four months following the referendum. They had lost most of their accounts as the Islamic government confiscated the private companies. The Ministry of Finance was informing them of the loss of another auditing account.

Kamal pulled open his drawer and took out a list of forty-six names. His eyes ran down the paper. There was just no way of avoiding what had to be done. His thoughts were interrupted by a soft knock. Rashid's head peered from behind the door.

'Forgive me, Agha Kamal, for interrupting. May I come in?'

'Yes, of course.' Kamal placed the paper in the top drawer and closed it.

Rashid took a glance behind him before entering. The door clicked gently as it closed. 'I wouldn't trouble you normally, but there's something you should know.' Rashid spoke in a low voice.

'What is it?' Kamal's throat felt tight. He offered Rashid a chair, but the security guard hesitated, before accepting with a nod. He sat on the edge of the chair, ready to sprint off.

'There's a rumour that the partners have made a list of names of employees you wish to sack. In retaliation, Lenin is organising a strike.'

Hussein Lenin was one of the managers. Everyone called him Lenin because he wore his beard in the same fashion the revolutionary leader had. He was also one of the most vocal in his protests against the firm and its partners.

Kamal shifted in his chair. Rashid leaned over with his elbows pressing down on his knees. 'Agha Kamal, you have been very kind to me and my family. But if I don't join them tomorrow...well they can cause a lot of trouble for me.'

Kamal nodded. He understood Rashid was taking a big risk by talking to him. He grabbed the leather armrests of his chair and leaned heavily on them as he raised himself upright. He walked Rashid to the door and shook his hand warmly, then he stood at the doorway and watched Rashid go down the stairs. He walked to the adjacent office, where the door was partially open and two of his partners were discussing an audit they were about to do. Kamal did not knock as he went in.

'We need to talk.'

A few hours later, the partners emerged from their meeting, all in agreement as to their next course of action. A general meeting was scheduled for the following day.

The 106 employees of the firm filed into the third floor. They had pushed the tables to the side and rearranged the chairs into an arc. Some carried placards with slogans they had written using the company stationery. Several were noisy, rallying the others against their 'bloodsucking' employers. Some, like Rashid, watched them with a quiet acceptance.

The room fell silent as the five partners walked in. One of them carried a parcel of envelopes. Kamal walked to the dais.

'Thief!' a man's voice called out. This started fresh jeering from the crowd. The words stung. Kamal bit back his anger and waited until the noise stopped. He looked into the faces of his employees. Most he knew, some he had taught at university. He regretted not having taken the time to get to know the newer recruits.

Kamal cleared his throat before beginning the short speech he and his partners had prepared. 'You are all well aware that there has been a substantial decline in the volume of work.'

'SAVAK spy,' the voices called out.

'There's simply not enough work to pay for all of your wages,' Kamal pressed on. 'We have no choice but to let some of you go.'

'Liars! You're hoarding all the money in your Swiss Bank accounts.'

Kamal recognised Lenin's voice.

As the notices were handed out the room became noisy again with voices protesting from all directions. The partners had to yell the names out.

Kamal locked eyes with Lenin. Finally, the last name was called out. A thin smile slowly spread on Kamal's lips. Lenin's eyes widened. His name was not amongst the retrenched. All eyes turned to Lenin. Some of the ones whose names had been called out glared at him. One man sitting close to him stood and spat on the floor at Lenin's feet before leaving. Most of the others walked quietly out of the room. Lenin looked wildly about him and into the deflated faces of his remaining comrades. He walked over to where the partners stood in a circle.

'You have made a mistake.' He placed a hand on Kamal's shoulder, turning him so they were face to face.

'There are no mistakes.' Kamal looked at his partners in mock surprise. 'We had forty-six names and they have all received their termination letters.'

A few employees had lingered at the doorway watching the exchange. Lenin shot a nervous look at them. 'Why was I not retrenched?' he said.

'We see no reason to let you go.' Kamal placed a friendly arm around Lenin's shoulders. He spoke loud enough so the others could hear. 'In fact we have all been extremely impressed by your dedication.' He dropped his voice as if sharing a secret with Lenin. 'The way you are going, son, I would have no problem putting a recommendation forward for you to the partners.'

Lenin's face drained of colour. He shrugged Kamal's arm off and stormed out of the room.

'I think we've broken the back of this strike,' one of the partners said as they descended the stairs to their offices. But none of the men felt like celebrating; they all knew bigger battles were ahead of them.

Nina stood in front of the bathroom mirror pressing the buttons of her Islamic uniform through their narrow slits. The dark navy tunic sagged awkwardly over her shoulders and the harsh material irritated her skin. She studied herself in the mirror. She almost did not recognise the reflection that stared back at her. In the months since the Islamic Republic had begun she had changed dramatically. She wore no perfume or make-up, her skin stretched taut across her face. She looked down at her hands. Her once manicured nails were now stripped of colour and cut short. Before she left for work she pulled her scarf down to her hairline and tied the ends into a tight knot under her chin. She was careful to tuck in any stray strands of hair.

Every morning, Nina made sure the kids were dressed, had eaten breakfast and tidied their rooms before she left. Kooros primary school had reopened tentatively but its future was fragile. She walked into Behzad's room and started picking up toys and colouring pens off the floor. A handgun popped in the rubble behind the kitchen.

Pop. Pop.

Her shoulders jerked with every pop. She exhaled to regain her composure and bent over to pick up a drawing. Turning it over to look at it, her chest tightened. It was the same as all the others. Black stick figures with guns lying in pools of blood, angry blackened skies swirling above. No matter how many of these she saw, she never got used to them. Her tears stung the back of her eyes. She crumpled the drawing in her hand and threw it into the wastebasket.

Although it had been almost a year since she was dismissed from her position, Nina still drove to work every day. She no longer had a desk. Most of her colleagues turned their heads when they saw her, or made her wait for hours before they would agree to see her.

She spent the days walking aimlessly through the corridors in the Ministry of Health. Whenever anyone asked her why she did not stay home, she would square her shoulders and stubbornly answer, 'I have done nothing wrong. I believe I have a lot to contribute and I will not allow myself to be defeated by rumours.'

Her colleagues would shrug and walk away.

In the car she turned on the engine and allowed it to hum while the heater warmed up. She no longer carried musical tapes with her, for fear of being stopped and searched by the Komiteh. Since last summer, Khomeini had censored anything which led to the 'corruption and demoralisation of man'.

In August, she and Kamal had joined thousands who had massed to demonstrate against the restrictions placed on the press. One by one speakers had taken the dais speaking about the essence of the revolution: freedom of press, freedom of speech and freedom of thought. But the mullahs' street thugs, better known as 'zealots with batons', had dispersed the protesters, chasing them into the alleyways.

Nina shuddered remembering her last demonstration. She turned on the radio for some companionship.

'This is Radio Azadi. This morning the university students, in protest at the Shah's arrival in the United States, have raided the American Embassy taking fifty-two hostages. The hostages were handcuffed and blindfolded before being led to a basement room. Imam Khomeini has not yet issued a response to today's events. Earlier in the year, when the revolutionary guards had occupied the embassy, he had ordered them out.'

Nina listened to the news in disbelief as she drove through the graffitied streets. It seemed every wall had slogans painted across it: 'Death to America. Death to Carter.'

God help us all if they don't release these hostages soon, she thought.

That night pictures of blindfolded hostages with guns pointing at them beamed across television sets. The students held press conferences displaying the documents they had found in the 'nest of spies'. Outside the embassy American flags were burned in front of cheering crowds with placards 'When Khomeini fights, Carter trembles.'

Despite international pressure, and pleas from Prime Minister Bazargan, Ayatollah Khomeini remained silent about the release of the hostages. He had not instigated the storming of the embassy, but he recognised that the takeover of the embassy had great symbolism: the underdog bringing a super-power to its knees. It stirred a lot of nationalistic pride in the hearts of many who had supported the revolution. Khomeini described America as the 'Great Satan' which had been directing its power over Iran and used the situation to gain support for the proposed constitution of an Islamic Republic.

Having lost his last shreds of authority, Bazargan resigned.

'Good morning. You are listening to the BBC World Service. Yesterday Ayatollah Khomeini was confirmed as Iran's absolute ruler. In a referendum, almost sixteen million Iranians voted for an Islamic society based strictly upon the limits set in scripture. The referendum comes almost a month since the storming of the American Embassy in November and the taking of the American hostages.

'In the White House President Carter has met with the women and black US hostages released from Iran two weeks ago. He warns Iran to release the remaining hostages or face the consequences. In response, Iran's Islamic radicals have warned that all embassy hostages will be shot on the spot if the US attacks Iran.'

The year 1979 ended with Ayatollah Khomeini being named *TIME* magazine's 'Man of the Year'.

The War

Virtues of the revolution

In Kamal's office, files and papers were scattered around him. A year before, in September 1980, Saddam Hussein sent his army across the Shatt al Arab river on the Iraq–Iran border and into land they claimed was rightfully theirs, thus declaring war on Iran.

Although initially surprised, the clerics soon realised that they could use the war to greater affirm their power and impose stringent Islamic rules. The ruling clerics mounted an increasing assault on the recently elected French-educated President Bani-Sadr whom they accused of being far too 'moderate'.

In March 1981 the Majles, the senate headed by political clerics, officially began to restrict Bani-Sadr's powers, accusing him of being a CIA agent.

In June, Kamal along with two thousand others, had marched in the street in support of Bani-Sadr and a secular constitution. Similar demonstrations had taken place in other cities. Enraged,

Khomeini thundered on national television, 'The day I feel danger to the Islamic Republic, I will cut everyone's hands off.' He stripped Bani-Sadr of his title and the former president escaped to France. With him went the last hopes of a secular government and the hope of assimilating Western democracy into Islam.

Kamal leaned back in his chair. He stared at the picture which he had become so accustomed to. The steely eyes, the eyebrows drawn into a crease on top of a long straight nose, the black turban and the grey full beard; Ayatollah Khomeini looked defiant. He found it ironic that Khomeini's picture hung from the same nail the Shah's picture had less than two years ago. So much had happened since those first days of the revolution. Nina had finally been offered a position in Iran's central medical organisation as the educational co-ordinator. She had moved from the Ministry of Health, where she had spent her days aimlessly in an empty room, to the education ministry where she was responsible for facilitating the education of the medical and nursing students. She visited schools, clinics and mosques as a health educator to teach personal hygiene, diet and family planning. Apart from the schools in Tehran she also visited the surrounding towns. She was content in her post even though it was a demotion for her.

In January 1981, 444 days after the storming of the American Embassy, the remaining fifty-two hostages were released. People didn't care about the hostages anymore. They had bigger worries to occupy them.

Every day a flood of refugees fleeing the border war with Iraq sought shelter in the capital, choking the streets and ghettos of Tehran. On almost every street corner old toothless women sat on cardboard boxes next to toddlers, extending their palms out for food or money. Most people walked by, avoiding eye contact. Sometimes the children ran after you, tugging at your shirt and pulling on your arm. Dark brown eyes that seemed too old for their youth pleaded for compassion. Scores of young men were shipped to the frontline, all with the promise of eternal youth in the gardens of heaven.

This morning Kamal had passed yet another death procession on his way to work. A group of thirty people dressed in black walked towards Behesht Zahra cemetery. An old woman leaned heavily on the arms of the people around her, her old frame too weak to support the heavy burden of her grief.

'Ali,' she wept, beating her chest with her open hands. 'How do I live without my Ali?' Behind her, a younger woman walked with a hung head. She held the hand of a small boy, and a baby was cradled in the folds of her black chador.

Worse than the death processions were the young men who returned from the front-line with missing limbs and the horrors of war in their eyes.

At night the city shrouded itself in a blanket of darkness. Windows with masking-tape crosses were veiled with heavy thick curtains. Street lamps and car lights were painted black. Every so often the sirens, followed by the rat-tat-tat of machine guns, saw people running to their basements, where they remained huddled until the all-clear siren sent them back to their cold beds.

Kamal sighed heavily and forced his attention back to his work. The firm's workload had doubled in the past year.

International firms that still had an interest in Iran insisted their auditing be done by people with Western credentials. The same officials who had kept them waiting for hours or refused to see them now greeted them warmly. In return, Kamal and his partners charged them premium rates.

There was a knock on the door. Azim's head popped around the door. 'You busy?'

Kamal, glad for a break, motioned his friend inside.

'Our house was broken into again.' Azim leaned on the door with folded arms and lightly brushed the new Islamic moustache he was sporting.

Kamal sat up straight in his chair. 'Again! How many times is that?'

'This is the fifth time,' Azim stretched out the fingers on his right hand. 'They just stole some food this time. I guess they've already taken everything they wanted the previous four times.' Azim's shoulders shook as he laughed at his own joke. He wiped the corners of his eyes before continuing, 'I'm going to get an alarm system. But they'll probably steal that too.' He laughed again, but stopped when he noticed his friend was not laughing.

'What's the matter, Kamal? You look tired. Is Saddam keeping you awake at night?' he chuckled, trying to get his friend to smile.

'I haven't been sleeping very well. I'm worried about the children. Behzad has started at the local public school. It looks like Banafsheh might be forced to do the same next year. She is coping all right, but Behzad seems to be struggling. He's up with Nina every night till nine or ten in the evening doing homework. He can barely see with the candlelight. He's still half-asleep when we drive him to school in the morning. He was caned last week for not having done his homework right.'

'Have you talked to his teacher?'

'You should see his teacher!' Kamal's jaw tensed as he recalled the meeting he had with the man. 'He's a 24-year-old thug with no formal education. The whole time Nina and I were in his office he was lecturing us on the virtues of the revolution and Islamic theology.'

Azim sank in the seat across from Kamal. He ran his fingers through his hair, tufts of which had greyed early. When he looked up a dark shadow had descended in his eyes. 'My situation is not much better. We're worried about our youngest son. He has started saying his *namaz* five times a day. But that's not what troubles us. He condemns me for drinking in my own home. He turns off the music because he believes it promotes Satan's ways. He gives revolutionary speeches. I now do everything in secret. I'm scared he might one day denounce me as anti-revolutionary.'

A pregnant pause descended between the two friends as each one reflected on the other's situation.

'Listen to me, Azim,' Kamal leaned across his desk. 'We've got to get our families out of this country. Do you hear me? We've got to get out! If Saddam doesn't get us with his bombs, Khomeini will by destroying our children.'

Just then Behrooz, another partner at the firm, stormed in. His face was flushed with anger. He slammed the door behind him. 'Those bastards! You won't believe what they've done to us.' He paced the room.

'You know how I want to visit my wife and children in London. Well, I went to get an exit visa and they told me I have seven stops in front of my name.'

Behrooz had married an English girl during his university years in England. After the revolution, his wife and their three sons had moved to England to escape the escalating anti-Western movement. Behrooz, however, had chosen to stay back because of his work.

'What do "stops" mean?' Azim asked.

'Since the start of the revolution, every time we do an audit for an organisation they put a "stop" in front of our name to prevent us from skipping the country in the middle of the assignment. Of course, none of them bothered to mention this point to us, or to lift it when the assignment was finished.'

'How are we going to lift these stops?' Kamal asked.

'I guess we have to start greasing some palms. In the meantime, I have to leave my home as collateral if I want to visit my family.'

Kamal sat motionless behind his desk with his fingers pressed together in front of his face. Behrooz's words still echoed in his head. None of the democratic rights he had hoped for during the revolution had eventuated. There had been a brief period of ease a few months after the Shah fled. But since then the censorship in the press and media had once again tightened. His *TIME* magazine had pages missing or black markers across pictures the censors deemed Satanic. Western movies were either banned or heavily censored. The curriculum in the schools was changing to include Islamic theology.

Kamal shut his eyes tight. It was a hard pill to swallow. When he opened them again he had already made his decision. He picked up his phone and started to dial.

I started the new term in an all-girl school at the end of our street. Within the first week my new theology teacher had berated me for being lax with my Islamic uniform. Never having had to wear a uniform before, I resented its shapeless form, and its drab grey colour. Risking punishment from my teachers, I would beg my mum to tighten the hem of my pants till they were almost skintight. I had torn off the last two buttons on my uniform so my skintight pants would show when I walked.

'Your chastity is not a frivolous issue,' she had warned me. 'You'll do well to remember that, young lady.'

One day after class she pulled me aside. 'Banafsheh, I have not yet seen you at our midday *namaz*. I want you to join us today.'

'But, ma'am . . .'

'But what? Your family does follow the prayers, do they not?' she asked, narrowing her eyes. People who did not follow the religious requirements of five daily prayers, as stipulated by Islam, were deemed *tagooti*. The last thing anyone wanted was for someone to cause trouble by denouncing them to the authorities as anti-revolutionary.

'Yes, of course,' I lied. 'But I was hoping to watch the volleyball match today.'

'What's important to you? Your duty towards Allah or your frivolous Western games?'

At lunch, twenty of us filed into the small assembly area after taking our shoes off at the door. In the corner, prayer rugs were piled against the wall. Each of us picked up one of the small rugs and a prayer stone and silently lined up in four rows facing Mecca. I tried to make myself as inconspicuous as possible. I stood close to the wall in the second row. I straightened my scarf, making sure there were no loose strands of hair. I had never performed *namaz* although I had often seen it at home or on televison. My mind raced back to all the times I had watched my Eshrat Mamman doing hers. Through the walls I could hear the laughter of the girls in the playground.

My teacher walked in along with the principal and three other teachers. She scanned the room until her eyes rested on me. She had brown almond eyes with full lips and high cheekbones. There was coldness behind her beauty. Whenever I gave the wrong answer to her questions her eyes turned to stone with disapproval. I smiled at her but she looked away as a roll call was handed to her. One by one the names were read out.

Our principal began the prayer. '*Besme-Allah Rahmane Rahim.*'

My lips followed in sync with the words. I fell to my knees, my forehead touching the stone from Karbala a second after everyone else. I sat up to find my teacher looking straight at me. We dropped down to the floor again. This time I was in time.

'Dear God. Please let it all go smoothly,' I whispered as my head rested on the stone again. I stood and flashed another look at my teacher. Her hands were open like a book in front of her. Her eyes were scanning the faces as her lips moved in time with the prayers. Once again we dropped to our knees and then to the floor. When we sat up again one of the teachers was walking between the students.

She was moving towards me. Two girls before me she stopped and asked a student to stand up and recite the prayers out loud. The girl did so without any difficulty. She then asked the girl next to me to translate the prayer into Farsi. Blood froze in my veins. The Arabic words were foreign to me. I kept my eyes straight ahead and tried not to show any of the panic that rose inside me. The girl next to me struggled with the translation. She stammered and stuttered before she started to cry.

'Go and wait outside the principal's office,' the teacher hissed at her.

The girl did as she was told, mumbling an apology between mouthfuls of air. She covered her mouth and nose with her hand to muffle her cries. The teacher watched the girl disappear behind the door and then turned to look at me. We were now standing for the final part of the prayer. The woman was the same height as me. I felt her eyes burning into me. A cold sweat formed on my back. I opened and closed my lips in time. Eyes forward. She walked in front of me, paused briefly, circled me once and walked back to the front of the room. I closed my eyes and exhaled.

Afterwards, I walked past the principal's office to go into the yard for the remaining ten minutes of lunch. I saw the girl leaning against the wall with her hands behind her. Her chin was dropped to her chest. She lifted her head as I walked past. Her face was streaked and red lines circled the whites of her eyes. Her eyes widened as she looked past me to the sound of approaching footsteps.

—m—

By the time Nina got home it was already dark. She had been to a school fifty kilometres out of Tehran. She had enjoyed talking to the young girls about the changes their bodies went through as they hit puberty, and heard their giggles when she drew a picture of a sperm and egg fusing to form a baby. She and her colleagues had stayed back after school to talk to the villagers about First Aid. She had shown them how they could dress wounds and sterilise utensils using vinegar. The village women brought their babies to her for vaccination. They told her how hard it was with their husbands off at war and how they had to queue for hours every morning in front of the bakery for their rations of bread.

The program was a continuation of a system set up during the Shah's regime. No one in the current government had bothered to axe it yet. And, ever since the war, everyone seemed too busy to check on what Nina was doing. As long as she filled out her worksheets with her hours, her boss did not interfere in her work.

Nina slowly turned the key in the door. She pulled her scarf off and ran her fingers through her hair. The house was quiet. A strip of light came from under Behzad's door. She knocked gently before turning the handle.

Her son sat behind the table dressed in his pyjamas with his head in his hand. His exercise book was open in front of him. Two candles burned on either side of his table. His eyes were heavy with sleep. He smiled weakly. 'Hi, Mummy. Will you help me with my homework?'

Nina's heart tightened. She exhaled, trying hard not to lose control. She walked over to the desk. 'How about you leave the rest and go to bed instead?' She began to close his exercise book.

'No. I have to finish it,' he stopped her and looked up with frightened eyes. 'My teacher will get angry if I don't.'

A large lump choked her throat, making it difficult to swallow. She forced a smile. 'I promise to wake you up early in the morning so we can finish it before school.' She removed his small hand and closed the book. She reached over and took one of the candles and blew out the other.

Exhausted, Behzad let her lead him to his bed. She tucked him in and stroked his hair. He fell asleep almost straightaway. The candle covered his face with an orange glow. His chest rose and fell in such harmony it was hard to believe he suffered from nightmares. Behzad rolled away from her onto his side. In the dim light of the candle she noticed dark lines on his white pillow. She touched the pillow with the tip of her fingers and particles came away with her touch. She leaned closer to the flame. A large crease formed between her brows. 'Oh my God,' her voice was stuck in her throat, 'he's losing hair.'

Outside, the sirens shrieked.

Looking for a way out

Kamal paced the waiting room. Azim was leaning back on a black vinyl seat with one leg crossed over the other, his hands deep in his pockets. They wore white business shirts with grey pants and no necktie. As part of the new Islamic attire all men had replaced their Western-style neckties with khaki jackets and facial hair.

A brown suitcase stood next to the chair.

The walls were bare except for a single picture of Khomeini. Two windows at the end of the corridor let in the breeze, along with the fumes of diesel fuel. From the street below came the relentless roar of car engines, their beeping horns and the occasional banging of a faulty exhaust pipe. The smog from the traffic trapped by the Alborz mountains added to the claustrophobic heat. It was close to the midday *namaz* and a loudspeaker somewhere outside was calling people to prayer.

Kamal paced to the open window and took in the view below. A car had fallen in one of the deep gutters that separated the traffic from the footpaths. A group of men had gathered around the car and were arguing about the best way to get it out. One of the back wheels had fallen in the gutter and spun pointlessly every time the driver revved his engine. Cars speeding past only just narrowly avoided hitting the bystanders, they beeped their horns loudly and hurled abuse at the men. Under different circumstances Kamal might have laughed at the scene.

'Kamal, sit down,' Azim patted the chair next to him. 'Relax will you!'

Kamal sank into a nearby seat resting his elbows on his knees. He laced his fingers behind his neck and stared at a spot on the floor. 'I spent half the night comforting Nina. She was hysterical. Behzad's losing hair from stress.'

He straightened up to look at his friend. 'I had not expected our lives to come to this,' he continued. 'Has it all been a pipedream? Was it too much to have wanted a democracy? To live in a country where we are free to be the masters of our own destiny?'

Azim put his finger on his lips and shot a nervous look at the assistant sitting behind the desk down the corridor. 'Please, Kamal. Lower your voice.'

Kamal shook his head. 'No. I feel I have let down my family. I didn't leave Iran when we could, and now . . .' his voice trailed off. 'And now the borders are closed and we have to beg to be released from stop lists.'

Just then the door to the office opened, a mullah and a tall man with khaki greens and a three-day growth walked out. The man in the khaki greens escorted the mullah to the door. 'Of course, Agha. Upon my eyes. Your wishes are my wishes.'

The man spoke with his hand pressed to his heart. He repeatedly bowed with a slight tilt to his head as a show of respect and deference towards the mullah. When the mullah was gone, the man turned to look at Kamal and Azim. He looked annoyed to see them there. 'Brothers, you have come on a very busy day.'

'We called yesterday to make an appointment. Your assistant told us to come before the midday prayers,' said Azim, in a relaxed, matter-of-fact tone.

The man looked at his gold Seiko. He tapped his watch. 'But I'm afraid it's time for my midday prayers now. Why don't you come back later, or would you like to say your prayers here with Abdul?' He pointed to a spindly man with a large nose and a receding hairline. Abdul had his prayer rug spread, facing Mecca. His stone from Karbala was placed at the top of the rug. His lips moved rapidly as he hooked his thumb behind his ears, raising his fingers and face towards Allah.

Kamal cleared his throat. 'We'll come back later.'

'Your wish is my wish,' the man said with his hand to his heart.

Winter was coming to an end and the weather was mild. I stood in line at the grocery store, clutching coupons firmly in my hand, waiting to buy milk, a carton of eggs and butter. Every so often the store opened and twenty or so people were allowed in. I had been standing in the queue earlier and had nearly reached the counter before I realised I'd forgotten our ration book and had to return home to get it. I was annoyed with myself when I'd rejoined the line that had stretched back around the corner. I flipped through the book. We had ration cards for different days. If we were late getting to the store we risked missing out as everything ran out early.

This was an especially busy time of the year. All over the country Iranians were preparing to celebrate *NoRuz*, the traditional Persian celebration of spring and the new year.

My grandmother wanted to bake sweets for when we had visitors coming to see us. It was customary for friends and relatives to spend the thirteen days of *NoRuz* celebrations visiting one another to wish a happy and prosperous year.

My grandmother had chided me when I'd returned for the ration book. 'When will you stop daydreaming, child? I will be shamefaced when the visitors come if I only have store-bought sweets to present to them.'

I knew if the store ran out of groceries before it got to my turn, Dad would have to try buying them from the black market.

The two women in front of me complained bitterly about inflation. They needed to buy new clothes and shoes for their families, plus presents for the kids. They shook their heads and clucked their tongues in disapproval.

I was restless. I'd often walked with my cousin to the store to buy chewing gum but, since the start of the war, the shelves were mostly empty. I craned my neck, checking to see if I could see anyone I knew in the queue. I recognised some girls waiting in line together. They were a few years older than me and lived in a nearby street, but I didn't know them well enough to try and push in with them.

A tall handsome man in his twenties walked up and down the line asking for milk coupons in exchange for rice ones. One of the women motioned him over.

'How many rice coupons do you have?'

'One kilo. I'll exchange it for two litres of milk.'

'Two litres? That is not an exchange, it's highway robbery!'

'Sister, this is a fair exchange. I have a young child at home,' he flashed her a charming smile.

'Don't call me sister. I'm old enough to be your mother and I wasn't born yesterday. One kilo of rice for one and half litres of milk, take it or leave it.'

'You're driving a hard bargain, sister,' he wagged his index finger at her.

She slapped his finger away. 'I have a good mind to report you to the Komiteh.' But she couldn't suppress a smile forming on her lips. 'Here, give me that coupon and take these for your "young child".' She handed him two coupons, each for a litre of milk.

'Charlatan!' she called out after him, nodding to her friend.

It was another hour before I left the grocery store. There were no plastic bags and I had forgotten to bring a bag of my own. I wrapped the groceries in my head scarf. It was only a ten-minute walk home and we lived in a tolerant area. I held the groceries gingerly against my chest, careful not to break the eggs. I was only a few metres from home when I heard a shout from behind me, followed by rapid footsteps on the road behind me.

'Hey you, where is your hejab?' It was a male voice but not mature enough to belong to a man. I quickened my step, resisting the urge to look behind me.

'You whore! You're an insult to the revolution and to Islam. Cover yourself up!'

My heart thundered in my ears as I ran the last few steps to the door. I buzzed the intercom several times. Every second felt like a lifetime.

I felt the stone coming at me before I felt its sting on my side. I doubled over, my hand automatically going to where the pain was.

'Take that as a warning.' I turned to see a boy not much older than me running into the opposite street. He stopped, picked up another stone and hurled it towards me just as I disappeared behind the safety of our gate.

'If I catch you again, I'll send the Komiteh to your house.'

My grandmother found me sitting on the stairs to our apartment, crying and clutching at my sides. The groceries were on the floor in front of me. Two of the eggs had broken leaving a yellow sticky trace from the gate to the steps.

After the meeting Kamal and Azim sat in Kamal's Buick.

'Do you think he will accept our "donation" in exchange for taking our names off the stop list?' Azim asked.

Kamal turned the ignition and pressed on the gas to warm up the car's engine. 'I don't know, he seemed very suspicious. At least he accepted the cash. Not like the last guy who told us they had no need for a briefcase full of money.'

Azim laughed. 'Yeah, I still haven't figured out whether he was too honest or just too dumb!'

'The latter most likely,' Kamal smiled back at his friend. He released the handbrake and eased the car into the traffic.

'This car is like a tank. How are you doing with petrol?' Azim asked, leaning over to read the fuel gauge.

Kamal reached into his breast pocket and pulled out his hand, it was full of coupons. 'I have enough coupons to last me two more years,' he laughed. 'Being able to charge these mullah organisations whatever we like has the advantage of keeping up with inflation. But no matter how much we can charge them,' the smile vanished from his lips, 'it still won't compensate for having to stand in front of that man and explain to him why we want our names off the stop list.'

They drove past a small shop selling paraffin. A rope extended out of the store, with people at the end of the queue passing it through the handle of their empty barrels and leaving them there until they would return several hours later. The line of barrels extended for a few metres. The men at the front of the queue dragged the barrels forward, they clanked loudly against the pavement. Since the start of the war paraffin had been in short supply and too expensive for most families to afford.

Azim stared at the queue of barrels. 'It breaks my heart to see my countrymen suffer like this.'

'This is no longer our country, Azim. We have to break our ties with it. Think of your family. We have to get our families out of this country at all costs.'

'What do you mean?'

'I mean, if we can't get these stops lifted then we have to think of other ways to get out.'

'What other ways?'

'We escape over the borders.'

'You can't be serious. There are bandits, and if the border guards catch you it could mean instant execution.'

They drove in silence for a few minutes.

'I can't live another day here,' Kamal's voice was barely audible. 'I can't raise my children this way. Everyday when I send Behzad to the care of that bearded thug my chest feels as if I've been stabbed with a knife.'

'How are we going to get out?'

'I don't know. But from now on whenever there is an audit for one of the banks at the border towns, we should go ourselves rather than send one of our staff.'

'Won't the staff become suspicious?'

'They never like going on those assignments anyway. Besides, we'll keep them busy with the bigger audits. All the same, this must stay hush-hush. We already have the Komiteh over every couple of days with some rumour of us skipping the country.'

Kamal turned into Azim's driveway.

'Would you like to come in for a while?' Azim offered.

'No. I've got to get going. We're visiting one of our friends tonight. They came back to Iran from the US after the revolution, thinking they were coming to a better country. Their eldest son was arrested at a party in a Komiteh raid two days ago.' Kamal shook his head and blew air out of clenched teeth.

'They picked up their son the following day from Evin Prison with fifty lashes on his back. He's seventeen.'

Hooshang opened the door to the apartment. A handsome man of forty, he was tall and lean with olive skin and thick black hair. He hugged Kamal and Nina affectionately.

'Thank you for coming. We've been so distressed since...' his words trailed off. He pulled a white handkerchief from his pocket and blew his nose. He motioned for Kamal and Nina to follow him.

'He wakes up screaming in the middle of the night,' Hooshang said as they walked down the hall to his son's bedroom. 'Faranak hasn't left his bedside all night.'

The door to the bedroom was ajar. Hooshang pushed the door gently open. Inside, on a single bed, his son lay on his stomach. He moaned between every breath while his mother gently caressed his hair. The flickering of the gaslight threw dark distorted shadows on the posters of rock stars decorating the walls.

Nina walked around the bed and took grieving Faranak into her arms. Faranak's face was wet and pasty. She pulled away from Nina and wiped it with the back of her hands. 'He's asleep. I've been giving him painkillers every four hours.'

Nina picked up the gaslight and lifted it over the wounds. The boy was covered with thick red and purple stripes criss-crossing his back. At times they had cut through his skin exposing raw flesh underneath. Nina suppressed the bile that rose within her.

'As Allah is my witness,' Hooshang's voice rose as he walked closer to the bed, 'I promise to find the animals who did this to my son.' He clenched his fist in front of his face. 'Then I'll kill them one by one with my bare hands.'

Kamal placed an arm around his friend and led him out. In the dark corridor, Hooshang dropped to his knees, buried his head in his hands and wept. 'I've failed my son, Kamal. I've failed him. I couldn't protect him from those animals. I brought my family back thinking I could provide a good life for them in our own country. All they were doing was listening to music. They weren't harming anyone.'

'Hooshang, the wounds will heal. You still have your son.'

Hooshang lifted his head. 'Kamal, it's not just the wounds. They robbed my son of his spirit, of his soul. They robbed the laughter in his eyes and the carelessness in his heart.'

Kamal turned away, blinking back his own tears.

The sirens shrieked. I woke up to the blackness in my bedroom. I blinked several times so my eyes would adjust. The sirens were followed by the rat-tat-tat of the machine guns. I pressed the palms of my hands to my ears, wanting to block the sound. I sat paralysed, staring at the veiled windows. Over the past months we had become used to the seamless blanket of darkness.

The door swung open. Mum stood in the door frame wrapped in a blanket, holding a torch. 'Hurry, Banafsheh. We've got to get to the basement.' She handed me my dressing-gown, wrapped me in a blanket and then pulled me into the living room where Dad was waiting with Behzad. Outside, I could hear the footsteps of the other families running down the stairs.

'Where's Mamman?' Mum asked.

'I sent her down with Mahin. Come on, we're taking too long.' Dad scooped a barefoot Behzad up in his arms.

Downstairs in the basement there were three rooms. The men had turned one room into storage for food supplies, while the second had a bed, extra blankets, clothes and some of our discarded toys. In the third they had set up equipment for brewing beer. All three rooms were always kept locked with the keys hidden. Behzad and I huddled with the other children on the bed while Mum and the women made hot tea on a portable paraffin stove. The men spoke amongst themselves in stilted worried tones.

'Kamal, have you heard the rumours?' Shapoor stroked the corners of his bushy moustache with his thumb and index finger as he spoke.

'Rumours about what?' Kamal scratched the area between his nose and his upper lip where he was growing a moustache.

Shapoor lowered his voice a little but kept it loud enough to be heard over the noise of the machine guns. 'A friend of mine said that in the south of the country trucks of revolutionaries drive around the streets. They round up children – young boys off the streets.'

'What for?'

'He says they use them as mine clearers,' Shapoor paused, swallowing hard. 'They give these kids a key. They tell them it's their key to the gates of heaven and then race them into the minefields.'

Kamal's throat went dry.

'It won't be long before they start rounding up boys from other cities. What are we going to do?'

Eide-NoRuz

The sun had not yet set in the sky. Everyone had crowded in the closed-off streets, where a row of dried prickly bushes were lined in the middle and lit into bonfires. The smoke from the bonfires made our eyes water. Bright ashes flickered from the flames as each person took turns jumping over them, singing: 'My yellow glow to you, your red flames to me.' Yellow was the symbol of sickness and the red glow of fire symbolised health and vitality.

Chahar Shanbeh Soori is a Persian tradition celebrated on the last Wednesday of winter before the start of *NoRuz*, our New Year. It dates back to pre-Islamic Iran to the Zoroastrian religion and has survived invasions and foreign rule.

In 1979, Khomeini had declared *NoRuz* celebrations void because it was not a holy day. Now, in March 1982, the radio had denounced *NoRuz* as a pro-Shah celebration. It had warned against lighting bonfires which would expose the city to Iraqi bombers. But, aside from a few zealots, people continued to celebrate *NoRuz* and bonfires were lit all over the country. As the sun descended in the sky the last of the bonfires died out and the sounds of *Allah-O-Akbar* filled the streets.

My cousins and I, along with other neighbourhood kids, covered ourselves from head to toe, including our faces, and with our flashlights took to knocking on doors and 'trick-or-treating' for nuts, dried mulberries, dates and figs.

Afterwards, we all met at my Aunt Mahin's place where they were having a party. The men had pulled out the alcohol from its hiding place and were drinking at the bar. The women sat around the lounge, gossiping and drinking tea. Dad walked over to Mum with a gin and tonic.

'No thanks, Kamal,' she raised her hand to stop him. 'You know I don't like drinking.'

'Go on, just try it,' Dad persisted, slurring his words.

Mum took the drink reluctantly. She took a sip and pinched her face at the taste. Dad laughed and turned back to join the men. Mum checked to see that Dad was not watching and placed the glass under the lounge. Somebody asked her about her job and she turned to answer, forgetting her drink.

I sat next to Behzad in a circle with my cousins. In the middle we had piled our booty and were distributing it between ourselves. On TV we were watching a video my cousin Zoya had borrowed from her friend which showed barelegged women and men in tight gold pants dancing to 'Grease'. Between mouthfuls of nuts, my cousin and I imitated the moves before falling over in fits of laughter.

It was well past midnight when our parents guided us sleepily down the stairs to our beds. I smelled whisky on Dad's breath as he leaned over to kiss my forehead. In that period just before drifting off to sleep I heard him stumble in the dark to the bathroom where he relieved himself while humming the new revolutionary national anthem. He washed his hands and teeth and grappled his way against the wall before falling heavily on his bed.

The shrieking of the phone jolted Kamal from his heavy sleep. He sat upright and fumbled for the phone in the dark. 'Allo?'

'Kamal, it's me, Ali Reza.'

Kamal leaned back against the wall. Ali Reza was one of the guests at the party. His and another family were the last to leave. Kamal reached for his watch on the bedside table. The fluorescent hands pointed to half past one in the morning.

'What is it, Ali Reza? Did you forget something?'

'No. I was following Davood home from the party. Suddenly, out of nowhere, a bunch of thugs in army greens and guns jumped in front of his car and stopped him. I managed to turn into a side street. I don't think they saw me.'

Kamal pressed his temples. He tried to think back to the past few hours. 'How much had Davood drunk?'

'Enough for them to smell it on his breath.' Ali Reza paused. 'They'd want to know where he was coming from.'

Kamal's throat went dry. 'How much time do you think we have?'

'An hour at most. I'm sure Davood would delay them as long as possible.'

Kamal went cold. He turned and looked at Nina. In the darkness he could make out her eyes looking up at him.

'Thanks for calling...no, there's nothing more you can do. I'll call you back. Goodbye.' He hung up the phone and reached for his trousers.

'Get up, Nina. Wake up Mamman, then intercom everyone in the building. The Komiteh stopped Davood,' Kamal spoke rapidly. He reached for the same jumper he'd worn earlier and pulled it over his head. It smelled of smoke. 'We have to clean up all traces of the party last night.'

Nina pulled on her dressing-gown and walked quickly down the corridor, switching the light on as she did. Most days there was electricity only for a few hours but tonight it had remained on.

Kamal switched on the bathroom light. He squinted against the brightness. His head felt heavy from the alcohol. He stumbled towards the sink and splashed cold water over his face. He looked in the mirror, his eyes were bloodshot with dark rings. He could hear Nina talking to Mamman. He shut his eyes and threw more cold water over his face, it eased the pressure inside his head and the nausea deep inside.

Upstairs at Mahin's, the women were busy clearing away all traces of the party. They sniffed the glasses to make sure no traces of alcohol had remained. Kamal collected the empty bottles and walked down the stairs to the building's main entry. He placed the bottles at the side of the building while he fetched a ladder from the garage. He switched the lights off and put a pen torch in his mouth to free his hands, then he placed the ladder under one of the downlights and climbed. Once he had unscrewed the base of the lamp, he gently eased out the light. There was a hole large enough to fit his arm into. He reached inside to feel where his secret stash of bottles were, then retrieved the empty ones from the side of the building and placed them inside the hole.

'God be willing, should I live to see tomorrow, I'll throw these empty bottles in the rubble,' he said to himself.

Once all the bottles were inside, he eased back the light and screwed the base in its place.

Upstairs, the music tapes and videos were hidden in the children's beds. There was nothing left to do but for each couple to return to their own homes and wait in darkness.

They did not have to wait long. They heard the cars racing towards them, gravel crunching beneath tyres as they screeched to a stop. Kamal pressed himself against the wall as he pulled back the black robe covering the window. His heart pounded high in his chest, and he could just make out the shape of two old Toyotas. The doors clicked as they were opened and men filed out of them. Davood was pleading with them.

'I swear there was no party. We get together with our families. I swear on the eyes of my ten-year-old daughter there were no boys and girls meeting tonight.'

'Shut up,' a gruff voice silenced him. 'You stink of Johnnie Walker. You're an insult to the revolution.'

In the darkness of the night Kamal could feel Davood shrinking. 'I told you before. There were some chocolates there. They tasted funny to me. They must have had alcohol in them and we didn't realise before we ate them.'

The man laughed. 'You hear that?' he called to his comrades. 'He says he's eaten chocolates.' Turning back to Davood, his expression hardened. 'I spit on your mother's milk. Do you think I was born yesterday?' He pushed Davood towards the gate. 'Call them. I want to try one of these chocolates,' he laughed again.

Davood pressed the intercom. Kamal moved away from the window. All the lights had been turned off but his eyes had adjusted to the darkness. He walked over to the corridor. Mamman and Nina stood in front of the intercom. Kamal motioned for Mamman to answer it.

She bit her lip. 'Who is it?'

'In the name of Allah, we are here to do our imam's work. Open up, sister.'

Mamman looked at Kamal who shook his head. 'What do you want from us? We're just families.'

'Open up!'

'But our children are asleep. Have some compassion. Come back tomorrow morning.'

'Now!'

Mamman looked at Kamal. 'Put on your chador,' he said to her.

'But Kamal —' Nina began to protest.

'They are not going to be heavy-handed with an old lady, especially a Haji. She'll be far more effective stopping them coming in than us.' He squeezed Mamman's shoulder reassuringly. 'Tell them you will be down.'

Mamman's fingers trembled as she took the receiver again. 'Wait there. I'll be down in a moment.'

Nina handed Mamman her black chador. Mamman slipped on her shoes and silently descended the stairs holding on to the rails for support. Kamal and Nina walked back to their bedroom where they watched from behind the curtain. Mamman's walk was laboured; her frame weighed down by worry.

'Haji *khanoom*. I'm so sorry to have bothered you at this time of the night, but these men think we were drinking here tonight,' Davood said.

'I swear on the Mecca I have made the Haj to, no one was drinking here.' Mamman bit down on her lip and prayed Allah would forgive her this lie.

'We will judge that for ourselves,' the soldier said.

Mamman turned the lock and slowly opened the gate. Davood was pushed through, followed by three Komiteh men in khaki greens and machine guns. Mamman drew a breath at the sight of the guns. A couple of policemen filed in after them.

'No need to worry, Haji *khanoom*. We mean you no harm,' one of the policemen tried to reassure her.

The Komiteh men knocked loudly on the upstairs door. From the darkness of their apartment, Nina and Kamal heard Mahin open the door.

'There was no party here,' she protested meekly.

'We will be the judge of that, sister.'

'Don't go there, we have young children asleep.'

Goosebumps popped on Kamal's back as he heard the men's footsteps walking through the apartment.

'How old are your kids?'

'They're only children,' Salman pleaded.

'How old?'

'Twelve and seven. Here's a photo of them,' Salman said.

'Who did you have here?'

'Just my brothers, my sister and two other families,' Mahin said.

'No singles?'

'No. We're all families with young children.'

'Did you serve alcohol?'

'I told you they were chocolates,' Davood stepped in.

'I told you to stay quiet, Johnnie Walker, or I'm taking you to the Komiteh headquarters.'

'Look for yourself. There is no alcohol here,' Mahin offered.

There were more footsteps as men walked through the apartment.

'Sergeant,' the Komiteh man called out, 'you stay here and search the place. Report to me if you find anything. I'm taking my men back to our post.'

The men's heavy footsteps descended quickly down the stairwell.

'Why did you let them off so easily?' Kamal heard one of them ask on the stairs.

'There would have been plenty of parties tonight. I'd rather sink my teeth into a juicier case than drag in front of the mullah a middle-aged couple with their sleepy children.'

Upstairs, the sergeant and his aide continued to search the apartment. 'We apologise for the lateness of the hour. We'll try not to hold you any longer than necessary,' the sergeant said. 'Please turn on your video.'

A few seconds later the sound of 'Top of the Pops' filtered down to the apartment. Kamal squeezed his eyes shut, remembering how scantily dressed the dancers were.

'I have seen enough. Turn it off.'

'I can explain,' Mahin said in a shaky voice as the television was switched off.

'Sergeant,' the second policeman interrupted, 'I think you should see this.'

The footsteps went into the corner of the lounge room. 'It smells like alcohol, sir.'

'Where did you find it?'

'Under the lounge, sir. It's still full.'

Nina's hand went to her mouth. 'Oh my God, that's my drink. It must have been missed during the clean-up.'

There was a moment of silence. Kamal rubbed his palms along the length of his legs. Nina reached up and took his hands between her own deathly cold ones.

'Thank you, officer. You have done a great job. Please wait for me outside.' The sergeant waited as the officer left the apartment.

'Please, sir, we have young children. We are no threat to the revolution,' Davood pleaded. 'We promise never to touch another drop of alcohol. Please, for the love of Allah, let this go.'

The sergeant remained silent. Mamman began to cry. Nina covered her face in her hands.

'Haji *khanoom*,' the sergeant said, 'take this drink and pour it down the sink. And in the future, please be sure your children are more careful in following the laws of Islam.'

'Thank you. May Allah protect you,' Mamman sniffed.

'Sergeant, wait please,' Salman's footsteps rushed into the bedroom and returned a few seconds later, 'please accept this as part of our gratitude.'

'No. My duty is to serve Allah. Give that money to the poor. They need it more than I do. Allah be with you.' The sergeant pulled the door gently behind him as he left.

None of the adults spoke about the night after the party. My cousins and I, with bellies full of sweets and hearts filled with happiness of new toys and clothes, had slept soundly. The next day other kids in the street told us what had happened. It frightened me to hear that the Komiteh had been to our house. I knew drinking alcohol and watching banned videos were serious crimes and branded our families as *Tagootis*. When I asked Mum about it she told me nothing had happened. I didn't believe her. I noticed how her jaw tensed and her lips paled when she answered me.

We soon grew accustomed to our parents' vague responses, especially in the months to come as all our lives became more shrouded in secrets.

Bazaar-e-Tehran

In Iran the taxis are shared by as many as six passengers heading towards a similar destination, which was dictated by the taxi driver. At times you had to change taxis two or three times before reaching your destination.

'*Koja?* Where to?' the driver shouted to some people waiting. He had to shout out the open window in order to be heard through the roar of traffic.

A few people yelled out different addresses and the taxi driver chose three of them.

'*Chand?* How much?' one of the guys asked, his head and shoulders inside the car.

'Fifty tomans,' the driver said.

The young man and his friend threw their hands up in the air in mock disgust. 'That's not a fare, that's highway robbery!'

'Get yourself another taxi then,' the driver retorted and pretended to drive off. This dance of negotiation continued for a few more minutes before a fee was agreed on and the new passengers got in. Two men squeezed in the front and a young woman got in the back with us. The windows fogged, enclosing us from the outside.

'Eshrat Mamman,' I asked, 'why do Iranians celebrate *NoRuz*?'

My grandmother and I were sitting in a taxi on our way to the bazaar.

'Well, *modar joon*,' she began, as was her habit whenever she explained something to me, '*NoRuz* dates all the way back to the Achaemenid Empire. It's an old Zoroastrian tradition that celebrates the holy elements of fire, earth and water.'

'Yes. But why do we celebrate it?'

'Because we are celebrating the exact moment the sun crosses the equator and equalises night and day. It is the celebration of life. We renew ourselves like the dawning of the new day. That's why we jump over the fire. To renew ourselves and to take from it the healthy red glow. We wear our new clothes and shoes and we spring-clean our homes, so everything would be fresh and new.'

'Why do we set the *Haft Seen*?' I asked her, thinking about the *sofreh* which is spread to celebrate *NoRuz*. The *sofreh* includes seven features beginning with 's', pronounced 'seen' in Farsi.

'What's with all these questions all of a sudden?' she laughed.

I shrugged my shoulders. 'I don't know. I guess I never thought about them before.'

'*Modar joon*. The *Haft Seen*, like the *Chahar Shanbeh Soori* and *NoRuz*, also dates back to the Zoroastrian period. Although I can't be sure, I think seven has always been considered a lucky number. Everything in the *Haft Seen* symbolises life, or wishes we have of life.' She counted the number of 'seen' that are in the *Haft Seen* one by one on her fingers.

'First we have *sabzeh* which is new growth. Then it's the *sonbol*. The hyacinth represents beauty, spring and new life.'

The taxi suddenly braked hard, throwing us forward. The driver tooted his horn and leaned out the window to hurl abuse at another driver. Eshrat Mamman squared her shoulders. Her lips parted as if she was about to say something to the driver, but she thought better of it and eased back in her seat.

'Now where was I? Oh yes, the *Haft Seen*.' She counted her third finger. 'So we have *sabzeh* and *sonbol*. Then comes *seeb*. Aside from adding colour and vitality, apples were the first fruit in the Garden of Eden.'

'But didn't Adam have to leave Eden because he ate the apples?'

'Yes, child. That's true. But the Garden of Eden is thought of, in our folklore, as the spring of life. And maybe...' she paused, 'maybe the apples are there to remind us not to sin.'

Outside, the streets of Tehran sped past in a collage of shapeless, edgeless colours, with its traffic, pedestrians and graffitied walls. I moved closer to my grandmother linking my arm through hers. She counted her fourth finger.

'Then we have *sekeh*. The coins, of course, are for wealth and prosperity.'

She stopped abruptly. Leaning forward she tapped the taxi driver's shoulder. 'Where do you think you're going? Why are you taking the long way? Are you hoping to get some more money from me? Do you think I'm not paying attention? Turn right into the next street. I've been travelling this route longer than you've been alive. Shame on you! Trying to play a trick on an old woman.'

'*Khanoom*, I have given you a very good price considering how expensive petrol is these days,' the driver said, turning his head and smiling at her in the hope he could charm her.

'Just remember I will not give you a single rial more than what we agreed,' she said and sank back into the seat. 'Now where was I? Oh yes! Next is *seer*. The garlic is to ward off sickness and bad omens. And *samano* is a brownish thick paste traditionally used in feasts.'

I pinched my face. 'I can't imagine anyone finding *samano* tasty.'

Eshrat Mamman grabbed my chin and shook it affectionately. 'Don't pinch your face like that. One day it will set pinched and no one will want to marry an ugly pinch-faced girl. As for *samano*, it's very nutritious and we should always be thankful for God's food.'

The taxi stopped and the two friends got out. A few people asked where the taxi was headed and finally a grey-bearded man with a set of rosary beads wrapped around his fingers got in the front seat.

'*A-salam-o-Aleykum*,' he said, bowing his head respectfully.

'*Aleykum salam*,' Eshrat Mamman returned the greeting. She then continued to count on her fingers. 'For the last "s", we can have *sumac, senjed*, or *serkeh*. They all add flavour to our meals.'

'What about the goldfish, the bread and the coloured eggs? None of them start with "s". Why do we have them?'

'My goodness, child!' She ran her fingers over my head and kissed my forehead. 'I was getting to that. Doesn't that daughter of mine teach you any patience?' Creases around her eyes deepened as her lips parted into a smile.

'The bread is there as our wish never to go hungry. The eggs are there as a sign of life and fertility; colouring them gives the table a festive look. The goldfish represent the animal kingdom. We need them for food and like us they are God's creatures. Now, tell me, have you ever watched the goldfish the second before the New Year?'

'No.'

'Just before the *NoRuz*, the fish stay perfectly still. As soon as the *NoRuz* begins they start moving and if you look carefully at them, you'll see they are dancing.'

I looked back at her wide-eyed.

'So, tell me do you know what else we have in our *Haft Seen*?'

'The Koran,' I said proudly. 'And Mum puts new tomans between the pages. She says it brings prosperity if it's blessed by the Holy book.'

'Excellent,' she chuckled. 'Families who are not Muslim include The Torah or The Bible. Can you remember what else?'

My brows drew together in concentration. A woman sitting next to me in a black chador leaned her head close to mine and said, 'Candles and a mirror.'

'Candles and a mirror!'

'Bravo! Now what are they there for?' Eshrat Mamman wiped the condensation on the window with her sleeve, scanning the street. It was busier this end of the city. There were many pedestrians with bags in their hands going in and out of shops.

I looked at the woman next to me. She was in her early twenties with dark almond eyes. Her eyebrows were plucked and shaped into an arch. She wore black eyeliner and mascara, but no lipstick. 'Candles are for fire and the mirror is to warn us by reflecting evil,' she said softly in my ear.

Eshrat Mamman smiled at the young woman and me before leaning forward in her seat to tap the driver on his shoulder. 'Drop us off at the next lights please.'

The spring air was crisp as the last remains of winter gave way to longer, sunnier days. The streets and footpaths outside the bazaars were crowded with shoppers and vendors haggling over the price and quality of what was being sold. Smaller vendors, with carts they pushed along, sold boiled broad beans and beetroot.

Inside the bazaar, a domed ceiling with sunroofs framed narrow corridors where shopkeepers sold their goods. Small fans suspended from the ceiling turned lazily, mixing the aroma of spices and foods into a thick paste-like air. The walls were decorated in faded mosaic tiles and the skylights on the roof allowed in natural light. During the blackouts the vendors used gas lamps for extra light.

Along the nearest narrow corridor vendors sold produce from the countryside, still smelling of the earth. Fresh herbs and dried spices were displayed in straw-woven baskets stacked on top of wooden boxes. Others sold vases, samovars and mirrors with elaborate baroque designs. Further along the corridor were jewellers and carpet-sellers.

The merchants wore crumpled suits with open-necked shirts and gold chains. They balanced their jackets over their shoulders, tugging at them occasionally to stop them from slipping off.

With my hand clasped tightly in hers, Eshrat Mamman sped past the stalls. I was drawn in by the colours and smells around me, and every so often Eshrat Mamman would pull at my hand, urging me to walk faster. I looked around me at the people and vendors with wide-eyed enthusiasm. I rarely went to the bazaars. Mum generally took us to the 'Passage', the new arcades that resembled Western shops. When we did go to the bazaars it was to the shoeshops where our feet were measured and shoes made for us. Or to dressmakers where we chose clothes from a variety of *Vogue* patterns.

A trip to the bazaar was an oasis of sound and smell. Vendors called out, advertising their goods to the shoppers. I was slowing my grandmother down as she pulled me behind her.

'Keep moving, child. The rate we're going *NoRuz* will have finished before we even begin our shopping.'

We reached a square where merchants were selling barley and wheat-shoots decorated with ribbons, along with goldfish, coloured eggs and hyacinths. The men were rural farmers with weather-beaten skin, faded khaki jackets and dirt under their fingernails. 'Pink and white hyacinths!' one yelled. 'I have hyacinths for your *Haft Seen*.' Shouts came from different stalls. 'Goldfish, fishbowls! Get your goldfish from here,' and 'Beautiful *sabzeh*! Coloured eggs! Get them today!'

We stopped at the first stall. Eshrat Mamman pulled herself up onto the balls of her feet, trying to see over other people's shoulders. She squeezed forward after one woman left, dragging me behind her.

'What can I get for you, *Khanoom*?' the vendor asked, but before my grandmother had a chance to respond he called loudly over her head, 'Get your coloured eggs here.' Hoarse from shouting, the vendor cleared his throat before asking again, 'What will it be, sister?'

Eshrat Mamman stiffened at being called sister. 'Let me see your hyacinths. What colours do you have?'

'White and pink hyacinths to add joy to your *Haft Seen*,' the merchant called out again into the crowd.

'Oye. Are you talking to me or to the crowd at the other end of the bazaar? You've deafened me with all your yelling! Give me a bunch of your mixed coloured hyacinths.' Eshrat Mamman pinched her face as she turned the flowers in her hand. She placed them close to her face and drew a deep breath.

'They don't even smell. How much do you charge for this rubbish?' Eshrat Mamman always criticised everything she wanted to buy in order to drive down the price.

The vendor smiled broadly, his upper lip disappearing under his bushy moustache. 'These are the best quality flowers. I've handwatered them myself.' He spoke with his hand on his heart. 'The aroma of these flowers will spread all over your house, making you drunk with their scent.'

'Huh! Such web of lies you people weave. Give me three bunches and pray Allah will forgive you for this daylight robbery.' She tucked the flowers into her plastic bag before grabbing my hand and pulling me behind her. At the next stall Eshrat Mamman had me pressed between herself and the merchant's crates of lettuce. The splintering wooden crates still smelled of soil and were filled to the brim with produce.

The merchant's hands were stained with dirt. A woman and two young boys helped him with his customers. Eshrat Mamman was bargaining over the price and quality of his produce. From where I stood I had an unobstructed view of the adjacent stall. I tugged at Eshrat Mamman's sleeve. She was in her element haggling over the price and took no notice of me.

'Mamman!' I tugged harder. 'Mamman, can I go over and take a look at the goldfish please?'

'No, child. It's not safe here with all these men around. They might grab you and then how will I answer your father?'

'Please, Mamman.'

She reluctantly agreed after making me promise not to speak to strangers.

At the fish stall I pressed my face close to the rows of glass bowls where the larger goldfish were displayed. The smaller fish swam together in buckets, most of them orange and unimpressive. Every so often a man with a hoarse voice and long nose used a fishnet to pull one out. The goldfish jerked and twisted in the net until dropped unceremoniously into a plastic bag filled with water. Amongst the ones displayed in the bowls, one stood out from the rest. It was large and white with a streak of orange across its body. Her fins spread gracefully as she circled around the bowl. I imagined her as a princess trapped in the body of a goldfish by a cruel wizard, her elegance masking a broken heart.

'Agha! Agha! How much for that goldfish?' I asked.

'Which one?' he said gruffly.

'That one,' I pointed. 'The big white one. The pretty one that looks like a princess.'

He didn't answer me, dismissing me as a nuisance.

'Agha! Agha!' I tapped him on the arm at the same time Eshrat Mamman joined me.

'Why don't you answer the child?' Eshrat Mamman snapped at him.

The man turned, irritated. His face softened into a smile when he saw Eshrat Mamman's hands laden with shopping, and the fine material of her scarf.

'A thousand apologies, sister,' he said. 'Now, little sister,' he turned to me, 'which one of these goldfish did you want?'

On the way home we sat in a taxi with an orange vinyl interior and a picture of Khomeini on the dashboard. We were crammed in the back between a mother carrying a baby who kept trying to pull her scarf down, and a young man with patchy facial hair. I carried my goldfish proudly, holding it up so the sun could reflect through the fins.

'*Tagooti!*' the young man hissed.

Eshrat Mamman clucked her tongue. 'Boys these days have such little manners.'

'You and your Shah-loving traditions,' the boy hissed. 'Our Imam has deemed all non-Islamic holidays anti-revolutionary,' the boy recited the well-rehearsed speech, pointing to the picture of Khomeini.

'Bah! You're not old enough to have grown a beard and your breath still smells of your mother's milk. What do you understand of revolution? Or of tradition?' Eshrat Mamman retorted.

The boy straightened up and pressed his chest out. 'I know this much. Your days, along with your old *tagooti* ways, are numbered.' He tapped the driver on the shoulder, 'Let me out here. I don't want to share a taxi with people who insult our glorious revolution.'

The taxi stopped promptly. The boy spat at my goldfish before getting out.

Kamal lay on top of the bedspread with his hands behind his head, and his thoughts filled with the events of the past few weeks. The afternoon sun threw strips of light and shade across the bedroom. He could hear Nina cleaning the bathroom cupboards. She had been spring-cleaning for the past two weeks. He closed his eyes and inhaled deeply. He heard Nina's footsteps entering the bedroom.

'Kamal, are you asleep? Lunch will be ready in a few minutes.'

Kamal opened his eyes reluctantly. 'No. I was just hoping I could close my eyes and open them to find us somewhere far away from here.'

Nina's eyes softened. She sat at the edge of the bed and took his hand. 'I know this past year's been frustrating for you. But something is bound to come up. We'll get to start fresh some place else.'

Kamal swung his legs over the edge of the bed, and ran his fingers through his hair. 'Well, so far our efforts have proven futile. Everything we've tried has led to a dead end. Worst still, whenever we go to parties the topic of discussion is our plan to escape. It's become ridiculous!'

'What do you suggest we should do?'

Kamal faced Nina. 'I've been giving this a lot of thought. We have to change our approach or it will get far too dangerous for us to leave. We tell everyone our plan has changed and that we are not going. This time we will plan it in complete secrecy. The only people who need to know at this stage are my business partners. The rest we will decide on a need-to-know basis.' He took Nina's clenched fingers between his hands and gently kissed them. 'From now on no one must know about our plans, not even the children.'

We sat around the dining table in our brand-new clothes and shoes. Behzad and I fidgeted impatiently in our seats. Mum had spent the last couple of days decorating the *Haft Seen*. The table was lit with candles which threw flickering shadows against the white walls.

In the middle of the table stood a large mirror with a handcrafted silver frame. Two matching candleholders stood on either side of it. An open Koran with gold-rimmed pages lay in front of them. Mum only brought these out once a year for *Haft Seen*. Every year, with her eyes lifted towards heaven, Mum reminded me that she was keeping them for my wedding *sofreh*. She always talked about my wedding *sofreh* with her eyes lifted towards heaven.

Mamman put brand new tomans between the pages of the Koran, which she later distributed amongst her grandchildren.

The rest of the table was decorated with barley shoots, coloured eggs, fruit, hyacinths, and other colourful features of the *Haft Seen*. Radio Azadi from America was playing music in the background.

At the completion of the song the announcer declared that there were only five minutes left to the New Year.

My goldfish swam in its crystal bowl. I watched it with deep concentration to see if what Eshrat Mamman had said about goldfish staying perfectly still at the moment of New Year would come true.

'Two minutes to New Year,' the woman announcer said over the radio. Mum took Dad's hand between both of hers. She gave him a warm smile.

'One minute to New Year.'

We sat silently.

'Ten seconds.'

Then the tick-tock of a clock as the countdown began.

'Ten . . . nine . . . eight . . .'

Mum's eyes grew moist. She squeezed Dad's hand.

'Seven . . . six . . . five . . .'

'Sit straight, child,' Mamman tapped my arm. 'Otherwise you'll stay hunched for the rest of the year.'

'Three . . . two . . .'

I looked at her with wide eyes.

'But I want to . . .'

'Shee,' she pressed a finger against her lip.

'One . . .' a pause and then a big gong was sounded, followed by the announcer's voice welcoming the New Year to her listeners.

Mum pressed her lips against Dad's. Next she embraced us hard against herself and held us that way until Behzad began to wriggle. We all then embraced our grandmother and wished her a happy *NoRuz*, then Behzad and I opened our presents.

As I climbed into bed that night I realised I had missed watching the goldfish when the gong of the New Year had sounded.

Seezdah Bedar is the thirteenth, and final, day of *NoRuz* celebrations. Tehran becomes deserted as people make day trips to the rural countryside to picnic. Cars packed with passengers and pots of food crawl along the jammed roads.

It was a warm and sunny spring day. Our families had decided to have our picnic in the front yard so the women would not have to bother with the hejab. After lunch the men had retired for a siesta and, after clearing the dishes, the women had joined them.

We children remained playing in the yard. My cousin Zoya and I tied knots in the grass blades, a tradition carried out by unmarried girls, and giggled over whom we wanted to marry.

'When I grow up I want to marry Luke Skywalker,' I said.

'And I'll marry Andy Gibb,' Zoya replied, giggling.

Zoya had a subscription to a French teen magazine. Unlike its English counterparts, the French magazines largely escaped the censors' black markers. We were spread out on the lawn flipping through the magazine when we were startled by the sound of gunfire and smashing glass.

We froze, pressing ourselves flat against the grass. My heart thumped rapidly against my T-shirt. I was so frightened. I couldn't tell the direction of the shots but they seemed very close.

Bang. Bang. Bang.

My younger cousins had hidden between the garage wall and Dad's car, with their skinny knees tucked into their chests and their palms pressed over their ears. There was a rush of footsteps as our fathers came running down the stairs carrying batons, followed by our mothers. Their faces had the shock of people awoken in fright.

The shots stopped and we ran to our parents, burying our faces in our mothers' breasts.

'Where are the other kids?' Dad asked in a panicked voice.

Zoya and I, unable to speak, pointed to the Buick. The men moved slowly towards the back of the garage. They held their batons, which seemed pathetically useless in the event of fresh gunfire, stiffly in front of them. They stopped when they saw frothy gold liquid spreading across the garage floor.

'Kamal,' Salman tapped Dad on the shoulder. 'You don't think it was the...'

'We'll soon find out,' Dad said.

The men remained still, listening. My cousins had crawled out from behind the car and run up the driveway into the safety of their mothers' arms where they shed hot salty tears.

'Who's there?' Salman called out. There was no response. A sticky liquid seeped from under the door next to the storeroom. Salman pulled a key from where it was hidden between cracks in the wall. He slowly turned the key and opened the door. Foaming beer washed over his shoes. He stared down at his feet and then at the scene before him in disbelief.

From where we stood we could see their shoulders shaking. Then we heard their laughter growing louder and louder. Dad walked back towards us, wiping his eyes.

'It was the homemade beer we've been brewing. It looks like we were a little too generous with the sugar,' he told us.

'You men and your beer-brewing scared us all out of our wits!' snapped Mahin.

Her comments sent Dad into another fit of laughter.

'Funny is it? A joke is it?' she said with her hands on her waist. 'See how funny you find cleaning that mess up.' She threw a broom at him before grabbing her kids and marching upstairs.

The men spent the remainder of the afternoon sweeping and hosing the beer and glass down the drain, and making plans for their next batch of homebrew.

Esmat

The phone rang, startling Kamal and Nina from sleep. Kamal reached for it in the dark, fumbling with the receiver before pressing it against his ear.

'Allo?'

'Kamal.' It was Azim. 'I think I found someone. And he seems genuine this time.'

Kamal looked at his Rolex. 'Azim, it's 11.30,' Kamal yawned into the phone. 'Shouldn't you be in bed?'

'I just got off the phone with him.'

'With whom?'

'I can't talk about it over the phone. Meet me outside of the old Chattanooga Coffee shop tomorrow at six.' With a click the phone went dead.

'Is everything all right?' Nina asked as Kamal hung up the phone. Late night phone calls generally meant someone had been arrested or was in trouble.

'I think so. That was Azim.' Kamal yawned again. 'The old man thinks he's 007.'

Old Chattanooga was a trendy coffee shop that had opened in the final years of the Shah's reign. Prior to the revolution couples used to meet there, but now it was only patronised by men. Along with landmarks and street names the coffee shop had been renamed after the revolution, but no one used its new name.

'So 007, are you going to tell me what's going on?' Kamal gave Azim's shoulder an affectionate pat.

Azim smiled meekly but his eyes remained serious. 'I think this one is the real thing,' he lowered his voice. 'I think he can get us out of Iran.'

Kamal felt a tingling down his spine. 'Who is he?' he asked nervously. 'And where did you find him?'

'His name is Esmat,' Azim said in a voice so hushed Kamal had to lean closer to hear him. 'He's from Turkey but he can speak fluent Farsi. Don't ask where I found him. I just did.'

Inside, the place was half full. Men sat in clusters or by themselves drinking tea and smoking. In the corner a noisy group was watching a game of backgammon between two rivals. Away from them, a man sat alone. As they got closer he looked up and smiled. When they shook hands Kamal ran an appraising eye over him. Esmat was in his early forties with thick dark hair that was brushed away from his face. When he stood, he was shorter than Kamal, with a round belly and manicured nails. After they ordered a fresh round of tea Kamal reached into his pocket for his cigarettes and offered one to each of the men.

Esmat rolled the cigarette between his fingers and ran it along his nose, inhaling the smell of dried tobacco. 'American!' he smiled and allowed Kamal to light the cigarette with his gold lighter. He exhaled smoke through his nose, almost disappearing behind its haze.

'You look for someone to take you out. Yes?' He spoke Farsi in a thick European accent.

'Yes,' Kamal answered, a little uneasy about meeting in such a public place. 'You know someone?'

'Yes.' Esmat smiled through a cloud of smoke and pointed the butt of the cigarette at his chest. 'Me!' He smiled confidently. 'It is my job. I help people get out of Iran.'

'When could you take us?' Kamal leaned forward.

'You decide when. I will take — no problem.'

Esmat leaned back on his chair and looked around the coffee shop. 'Nice here, no? Pity Shah go,' he said, drawing his eyebrows together and shaking his head in mock disappointment. 'But Khomeini,' he said with a quick smile, 'is good for business.' He laughed, blowing more smoke into the air.

The waiter brought another round of *estekans* filled to the brim with hot black tea. For half an hour, Esmat explained how he smuggled people out of Iran.

'One more thing,' Esmat stabbed his cigarette into the full ashtray, 'I get money from you in full one night before we leave.'

'How will we get in contact with you?' asked Kamal. 'I mean when you're away from Tehran?'

'I will give you address. You see Haj Ali Khan. If any news, he will let you know.'

Kamal pulled out his pen from his breast pocket, but Esmat grabbed his hand, all humour gone from his voice. 'You not write. You remember.'

'Esmat's quite a character, don't you think?' Azim said as he and Kamal walked briskly back to their cars.

'I feel a lot better knowing you guys will be there to watch our backs when we are on the mountains,' Kamal said.

'Well, actually, Kamal,' Azim slowed his pace, 'there's something you should know.' They stopped at Azim's car, and Kamal turned to face him.

'Mehry is pregnant. We just found out. I don't know how safe it would be for her climbing those mountains,' Azim spoke with downcast eyes.

Kamal's heart sank. 'So what will happen now?'

'I don't know. The pregnancy was an accident,' Azim said shyly.

'I can't wait that long, Azim,' Kamal said. 'I'll speak to Nina. If she feels we should go, we can go and then write back to let you know whether or not you should come the same way.'

There was a tightness in Kamal's chest as he watched his friend drive away. We will have to do this on our own, he thought, and for the first time in a long while he recited a Koran prayer his mother had taught him as a child to protect himself from danger.

I woke up early, stumbling half-asleep to the bathroom. I noticed a slit of light underneath the kitchen door. At first I thought nothing of it, but I noticed the light was still on when

I walked back to my bedroom. Thinking it must have been left on by accident, I decided to take a look.

The kitchen table was piled with butter, feta cheese, fruit and leftover food. Both of the double-sided fridge and freezer doors were open and Mum stood in front of them, pulling the rubbery edges off the doors.

'What are you doing, Mum?'

'What are you doing out of bed?' she asked, startled.

I picked up a red apple and started crunching on it. 'I thought someone had left the light on by mistake. What's all this?' I pointed to the table.

Just then I noticed another bundle. Thin strips wrapped in plastic and masking tape. One of them had been opened. I picked it up to take a closer look.

'There's jewellery in here,' I looked up to see another one sticking out of the rubber edge Mum was pulling from the fridge.

'Are you hiding these?' I asked.

'I think you should go back to bed.' Mum gently took the jewellery out of my hands and led me out of the kitchen.

'It's important you don't tell anyone what you saw,' Mum said in the hallway. I nodded, not fully understanding the trembling in her voice.

Kamal stared at the mechanic's shopfront where he was to meet Haj Ali Khan. Despite Esmat's warning he had written down the address as soon as he'd climbed into his car. He pulled the crumpled piece of paper out of his green army jacket, looked at it and looked back at the shop. Carefully, he folded the address and put it back in his jacket and then slowly pushed open the heavy glass door with bars at the front. The bell above the door jingled.

An old man with a tuft of white hair and a crumpled suit sat behind a low counter reading the paper. There was a faded Persian rug spread over the counter with a pack of Iranian cigarettes, a half-drunk tea and some papers scattered on top. The shop itself was no larger than thirty square metres, with a few car parts scattered around.

'Yes, please?' the man said without taking his eyes off the paper.

'Haj Ali Khan?' Kamal asked.

Haj Ali looked up from the paper and eyed Kamal suspiciously. 'Yes.'

'I'm Dastyari.' Then lowering his voice and nervously looking over his shoulder, 'Esmat sent me.'

Haj Ali folded the paper, placed it on the counter and stood to press a sweaty palm into Kamal's hand. 'Of course. Please have a seat,' he pointed to one of a half-dozen wooden stools scattered around his shop. He put his head through a door that led to a back room.

'Hassan!'

'Yes, Agha?' a young man's voice came from the back.

'Bring two teas, boy.'

A few minutes later Hassan, a slim man of thirty, brought two teas with a cup full of sugar cubes balanced on a dirty tray. He nodded a greeting to Kamal as he offered him a tea.

Just then the bell above the door jingled. A man's head poked through the door. 'Agha, do you have any gearboxes?'

Haj Ali made a slow motion with his head indicating that he didn't.

A few others came and went. Haj Ali, it seemed, had nothing to sell. Some customers stayed for a while. Hassan served them tea as they sat next to the counter. Kamal watched as they offered Haj Ali different sums of money for spare parts he did not seem to have. Others came to sell spare parts. Curiously, Haj Ali rarely bought anything either. He patiently listened to all offers as he nodded his head, uttered a lot of *Inshallah* and *Mashallah* and spun his worry beads. He would then answer them with the same motion of the head and a slow exaggerated 'No' before offering his guests more tea.

During the Shah's time, the shop was most likely a struggling business selling secondhand car parts. Now it seemed it was a booming business in people smuggling.

Kamal rarely visited the bazaar, except around *NoRuz* or when he needed new handmade leather shoes. His father had had a business in Tabriz bazaar and, as children, he and Jalal had spent a lot of time walking through the stalls. Sitting in Haj Ali's shop brought back memories of characters he used to see in Tabriz bazaar.

After two hours of sitting on the same hard seat, he was starting to get impatient. He had tried to look less conspicuous by wearing his green army jacket and an old pair of tanned coloured trousers. He kept touching his moustache, combing it down with his fingers. He had been served countless number of teas and shifted uncomfortably in his seat from a full bladder.

At one stage when there were no customers and Hassan had been sent on an errand Kamal leaned over to Haj Ali.

'Haj Ali Khan, I was sent here to see you by Esmat,' Kamal put a special emphasis on 'Esmat' in case Haj Ali had missed it the first time.

'Yes, of course,' Haj Ali said, exaggerating his 'yes'. 'And you are most welcome here. *Inshallah* you will visit us many more times. Give us the honour of having more tea with us.'

Kamal blew air out of puffed cheeks in frustration. He decided to try a different approach. He leaned over the counter. 'I have two small children,' he said in a soft voice.

'*Mashallah! Mashallah!*' Haj Ali said, nodding his head.

'It's very important for me to know what distance we'd have to walk,' Kamal pressed. Haj Ali gave Kamal a long look. He raised himself from his seat with some effort and motioned Kamal to follow him. About 500 metres from the shop was one of Iran's oldest cigarette factories. As a high school student Kamal had been through the factory on an excursion. Haj Ali placed a hand on Kamal's shoulder as if speaking to an old friend.

'From this spot,' he pointed to where they both stood and then to the factory, to there. 'That is all you and your family will have to walk. The rest you leave to us.'

Kamal felt a heavy burden of guilt and anxiety lift from his heart. Nina and the kids should have no problems walking that short distance. He left Haj Ali's shop with his head full of a list of things they needed to do.

Planning in silence

I stared at John Travolta's bright blue eyes. They reminded me of the colour of summer morning skies. He stood, half-turned, smiling into the camera in a tight-collared denim shirt. Mum had bought the poster for me and I had stuck it above my bed. I would have preferred Luke Skywalker but the only one the shopkeeper had was from the scene when Luke lassoes himself and Princess Leia to safety and I didn't want to share my bedroom with her.

Behind me sat Mum dressed in a smart wool-pleated skirt and a chiffon blouse. I had asked her to straighten my hair. She pulled the brush repeatedly through my hair with a heavy hand. Next to her on the bed she had laid out my best dress.

'Ouch. Not so rough, you're hurting me,' I protested.

'Stay still. You hair is full of knots.' Mum pulled the bristles against my scalp. 'I won't be able to straighten it,' she said in a resigned voice and dropped her arms. 'I'll have to pull it into a bun instead.'

I let out an exaggerated sigh. 'Where are we going again tonight?' I asked.

'I've told you ten times now,' she said, 'we are going to visit a friend of Daddy's.'

'Why are we going?'

'Because Dad's friend wants to meet all of us.'

'What does he do?'

'He works for the Australian Consulate.'

'Does he have any kids?'

'I don't know. He doesn't live here. He lives in Turkey.'

'But you said he's English.'

'Australian! But he lives in Turkey.' She pulled hard on my hair as she twisted it into a tight knot above my head.

'Ouch, Mum!'

'Sorry. Nearly done.'

'Mum, do Austrians know how to speak English?'

'Austwalians. And yes they sweak Engwish,' she said with a mouthful of hairpins. She dug the pins through my hair and into my scalp, then she spun me around to survey the result and smiled.

'What's Australia like, Mum?'

'I don't know, dear. Probably like England except with better weather.'

'Daddy . . . I mean Baba, said the man will ask us questions and we have to answer in English.'

Mum placed her hands gently on my shoulders and looked into my eyes. 'Please listen to your father. This visit is very important to your daddy and me.'

I nodded, looking down at my hands. 'What if the man asks me something about Australia and I don't know the answer? Will Da...Baba get mad?'

'No, Daddy will not get mad. Just answer what you can. Okay?' Mum kissed my forehead before getting off the bed and walking towards the door.

'I'm not allowed to call him "Daddy" anymore,' I said, staring at my hands on my lap. 'He's asked me to call him Baba. He said "Daddy" draws too much attention to us when we're out. He said the last thing we want is to get ourselves into trouble by being *tagooti*.'

Mum hesitated at the door and looked back at me with soft eyes. 'Times are different, sweetheart. We've all had to make changes.' She left my room, gently closing the door behind her.

We arrived at the apartment of Dad's friend from Australia a little after 8 pm. Dad shook hands with the man and called him Andrew. Andrew was much taller than Dad, and wore a pin-striped suit and a navy tie. He had to bend down to shake hands with Behzad and me when Dad introduced us. I shook hands with him timidly, not sure how I should act. Andrew ushered us to a room where the four of us crowded on a settee while he sat behind a large desk, making notes as he spoke to us.

Mum and Dad answered questions about their work. I found it odd that Andrew did not know much about my parents. He kept referring to a form on his desk before asking another question. Mum and Dad were very eager to please him, laughing at all his jokes even though they were not very funny.

At the end of our visit Andrew asked me if I'd like to live in Australia. I stared at him blankly, not knowing what I should say.

'She's a little shy,' Mum offered.

Andrew smiled then straightened to shake hands with Dad. 'Your application looks good, Kamal. I'll call you soon with the visa details.'

Dad looked relieved and stood up to take Andrew's hand.

'The visas would be issued from our embassy in Ankara,' Andrew said. 'With the borders closed, I trust you know people to help you with an exit visa.'

Kamal visited Haj Ali two or three times a week. Hassan was always there, making tea, running errands or just sitting quietly in the corner.

He also saw Esmat regularly. At their previous meeting Esmat had asked Kamal to bring his family's passports the next time.

'Why do you need them?' Kamal asked

'I leave for Turkey. I get you Turkish visa stamps.'

'How are you going to do that?' Kamal asked, not sure he wanted to trust Esmat with their passports.

'You accountants. You so simple,' Esmat gave Kamal a friendly pat. 'I fix things. I know people. You just need a little...' He rubbed two fingers against his thumb.

'How much?'

'For you my friend only 4000 tomans.'

After their next meeting, Kamal drove Esmat home. He handed Esmat their passports and money, and watched with disgust as Esmat shoved them down his pants.

'You visit Haj Ali for news. Okay?' Esmat opened the door and got out.

'Wait, Esmat,' Kamal leaned over the passenger seat, 'I'm taking my family skiing. I won't see Haj for a week after tomorrow.'

'*Inshallah* the passports will be ready by then,' Esmat said jovially.

Kamal nodded and pressed his foot on the accelerator. He did not wait to see Esmat go inside.

The next day Kamal visited Haj Ali Khan as had become his habit. He was surprised to find the shop closed and the blinds drawn. He tapped on the window. 'Haj Ali! Are you there?'

Haj Ali pulled back the blinds. He looked pale and anxious. He opened the door and motioned Kamal to come in, quickly locking the door behind him. Straightaway there was a knock on the door.

'Were you followed?' Haj Ali asked Kamal in alarm.

'I don't think so. What's going on?'

Haj Ali pressed his finger to his lips and with knotted brows pulled back the blinds.

'*Salaam*, Haj Ali. Did you get any gearboxes?' asked a man's voice.

'Are you blind?' snapped Haj Ali. 'Can't you read the sign, you illiterate! I'm closed. Come back next week.'

He pulled back the blinds and turned to Kamal, 'I've got bad news. They've caught Esmat.'

Colour drained from Kamal's face. 'How's that possible?' he asked in a hoarse voice. 'I drove him to his apartment myself.'

'They were waiting for him when he walked in.'

Kamal held on to the counter as he eased himself onto one of the stools. His head was swimming. He suddenly remembered something. 'Our passports! I gave our passports to Esmat just before he was . . .' his voice trailed off.

'Don't worry,' Haj Ali reassured Kamal. 'Esmat never carries any passports on him. He would have hidden them in a safe place before entering his apartment.' Haj Ali then turned to Hassan who was sitting silently in the corner and whom Kamal had not noticed until now. 'Boy, go make some tea for Agha Kamal.'

Kamal's eyes followed Hassan until he disappeared to the back of the store. A cold sweat hung to his back. 'Do you know what's happened to Esmat?'

'He's been taken to the border and expelled from Iran. More than that, I don't really know.'

'What will happen to us?' Kamal said, almost to himself. 'What if we don't get our passports back?' A sharp pain pressed at his temples. 'What if the police or the Komiteh guards search Esmat's house and find our passports? They will surely arrest us.'

'There is someone else.' Haj Ali eased himself onto a chair opposite Kamal. 'Esmat has a brother, Haales.' Haj Ali tapped his temple with his finger. 'He's the one with the real brains in the family. *Inshallah*, he'll take over the business.'

Kamal straightened, 'How long before he gets here?'

'Not very long. *Inshallah*, he'll be here in a few months.'

Kamal's heart sank. In the past few months he had been tidying up loose ends at work. He had found a buyer for the house and was currently negotiating the terms of settlement. Their application for Australian residency had gone through and last week the Australian consulate had invited them for an interview at his residence.

'Another few more months!' he whispered to himself and pressed his eyes shut in frustration.

I looked up and down the mountain for any patrol guards. The mountain was covered with heavy fog. Below, I could see two queues outside the mountain lifts: one line for women, the other for men.

Last year the ski fields had become segregated. The little red cabins took the skiers up and down the mountain. At the top a patrol guard directed the men and women towards different slopes. Most of the blue and black runs were on the men's side of the mountain, and after going up and down the green slopes on the women's side, I quickly got bored and looked for ways to get across to the other side.

I wore blue denim jeans, a navy windcheater that covered my hips and a black beanie. Once I pulled the ski goggles over my eyes I looked like a teenage boy. At the top I followed the women to the female side of the mountain. Then, about a kilometre down the slopes, I traversed the snow to the other side, swapping back at the end of the run. I had to be careful not to get caught by the patrol guards who were stationed along the slopes.

I had left Mum at the start of the run, agreeing to meet in front of our hotel for lunch, and skied down the mountain with a girlfriend.

'Where's your mum?' Dad asked as I finished the run.

I shrugged, 'She was too slow.' I clicked out of my skies.

'Didn't I tell you to ski with her?' Dad searched the slopes, scanning the skiers as they came down the mountain.

'I wanted to ski on the men's side.'

'What have I told you about doing that?' he said in frustration. 'Do you want to end up with fifty lashes on your back?'

I said nothing. He started to scan the skiers again. Two patrolmen were carrying someone on a stretcher. They were yelling at the skiers to get out of their way. Dad continued to search the mountain, muttering about how unreliable I was.

Behzad had started building a snowman and I decided to join him.

'I'm worried about your mum,' Dad said without taking his eyes off the mountain. 'You'd better go back up and ski down looking for her.'

I was clicking my skies back on when an announcement came over the speakers. 'Could Kamal Dastyari please report to the First Aid.'

Dad suddenly looked pale. 'That must be your mother. Take your brother up to the room.' He reached into his pocket and pulled out 100 tomans. He pressed it into my hand to buy ourselves lunch.

Dad found Mum at the First Aid with a broken leg. Mum's leg was in a cast for several weeks. Despite hours of physiotherapy, she dragged her leg behind her as she moved and used a cane to help her walk. I caught Dad a few times watching Mum hobbling around the apartment with a worried expression in his eyes.

It was now May 1982 and I was preparing for my final year exams. I had not done well in my Islamic Theology class. My teacher had warned me that if I didn't improve in my exam she'd make me repeat. But if I achieved a perfect score she would disregard my previous marks. I was lying on my bed writing cheat notes in English on tiny slips of paper and pinning them on the hem of my uniform. Next to my textbooks was an old edition of *LIFE* magazine. Dad still subscribed to *LIFE* because I enjoyed looking at the pictures. The page was open to a spread on the wedding of Prince Charles to Lady Diana Spencer. She wore an ivory wedding dress with a long train and puffy sleeves. The Iranian censors had blacked out the picture on the balcony of the couple kissing. I closed the magazine, trying to focus on my studies.

Instead my thoughts wandered to the events at home. Mum and Dad were acting curiously everyday. They spoke in hushed tones and spent a lot of time in their bedroom with the door locked, or making lists of things around the house: electrical goods, furniture, plates and cutlery, ornaments, books and our record collection.

One time I walked into their bedroom to find them both crouched in front of the safe. Mum was speaking to Dad in a tone of barely controlled anger because he didn't where the passports were. They stopped talking when they saw me.

Dad brought strangers to our home and walked them through the apartment. Some would return again with their wives. Behzad and I were always introduced to these people as 'my daughter and my son'. Dad was more polite than friendly with them. They generally stayed for only a few minutes, rarely accepting Mum's offer of tea. Afterwards, Dad walked them to their cars. I could see them from my bedroom window as they stood talking for a long time, pointing occasionally to the building. Dad looked as if he was reasoning with them.

Once, after a couple had gone, I asked him who they were and he said, 'Friends of your mum and me.'

'Do they have any kids?'

'I don't know,' he answered, distracted.

'I thought they're your friends.'

'Look, Banafsheh, you just have to trust me on this. Okay?'

I nodded, wanting to please him. He was tense and anxious and I didn't want him to be angry with me.

Haales

The bell above the door jingled as Kamal pushed it open.

Haj Ali lifted his head out of the newspaper. 'Oh, Kamal Agha!' Haj Ali clapped his hands. His face was animated as he walked around the counter to greet Kamal. 'I have good news for you...come now, sit down...Boy, bring Agha Kamal some tea.'

Kamal sat in his usual spot next to the counter.

'I have such good news for you,' said Haj Ali. 'Haales will be here today. Such luck you should come by today. Praise be to Allah,' Haj Ali turned his face and palms up towards heaven.

Kamal's eyes widened. 'When will he be here?' he asked.

'Shortly, *inshallah*! Rest at ease, he will be here.' Sticking his head through the back door, he shouted, 'What's happened to those teas, boy? Agha Kamal will die of thirst before you get your lazy bones to bring some tea.' He turned back and shook his head at Kamal as if to imply 'It's so hard to find good help'.

Kamal soon learned that for Haj Ali, 'shortly' meant anytime between now and a few hours from now. For the next five hours, Kamal sat on his stool, sipped his tea and smoked his cigarettes. Occasionally he walked over to the cigarette factory where he relieved himself behind a wall.

During this time men came and went just like other days. Haj Ali never bought or sold anything. He sat behind his counter, rolled his head back, clucked his tongue, stretched his 'no's, ordered more tea and waved the men away with '*Inshallah*, next time'.

After one of his walks to the cigarette factory, Kamal returned to find a man he had not seen before sitting on one of the chairs. Both Haj Ali and Hassan treated him with reverence. The man sat straight on Haj Ali's chair. His hair was cut short and business-like, and his moustache was trimmed. When he looked up at Kamal his eyes were dark and cold.

'Oh, Agha Kamal. Here you are at last,' Haj Ali said as he welcomed Kamal. He locked the door behind them and pulled down the blind. 'This is Haales,' he whispered in Kamal's ear.

Haales stood and extended his hand. 'I am Haales. Your acquaintance I am happy to make,' he said, taking Kamal's hand firmly into his own.

Kamal nodded, 'I'm Dastyari.'

Haales motioned for Kamal to sit opposite him.

'We were almost ready to leave when Esmat was caught,' Kamal began. 'In fact he had our passports with him.'

Haales reached into his breast pocket and pulled out two Iranian passports. He opened them, lifted his eyes to Kamal, and closing the passports handed them to him.

'All the time, they safe here with my wife,' he said in a clipped voice.

Kamal, surprised to see the passports, checked them before putting them away in his breast pocket.

'As I was saying, we were ready to leave...'

'I take you,' Haales interjected.

'When can we leave?' Kamal said, his heart beating hard against his chest.

'This week!'

'This week? But... but that's too soon,' Kamal stammered. 'That's impossible. We can't this week.'

'Okay, next week,' Haales said.

'I have to speak to my wife.'

'Okay. I leave one time every week. When you and wife ready, I will take.'

Haales stood abruptly and shook hands with Kamal and nodded to the other men before turning to leave. Haj Ali nearly fell over in his haste to get the door opened for him.

Kamal burst into the bedroom, 'We're leaving, Nina.'

Nina was reading on the bed with her legs stretched out. She dropped the book and looked at Kamal with wide eyes. 'What... when... calm down... start from the beginning.'

Kamal dropped to his knees next to the bed, took her hand and pressed it to his lips. 'I met Esmat's brother today. I'm telling you, he really means business.' Kamal got off the floor and started pacing the room. 'He's all business-like and has none of Esmat's showmanship. He said as soon as we pay him, he will take us.'

'How much does he want?'

'It's 80 000 tomans for us, and 20 000 tomans for each child.'

'Where are you going to raise that much cash?'

'On the way home I stopped at the bank where your brother works. I told him that I need 260 000 tomans in 1000 denominations.'

'Did he ask why?'

'Yes. I told him I'm buying a chicken farm.'

Since the revolution, Kamal had been involved in many business ventures, amongst them a courier truck business and a chicken farm.

'Did he buy it?' Nina asked, bemused.

Kamal shrugged his shoulders and smiled. 'I was very convincing.'

Nina fell silent. She stared down at her hands. Kamal stopped pacing when he noticed the change that had come over her. He walked over to the bed and sat beside her.

'What's the matter? Are you having second thoughts?'

'No,' she said, 'it's just...I feel terrible for not telling my mum.'

Kamal put his arm around her small frame and pulled her head onto his chest. He stroked her hair as he spoke, 'We've already discussed this. It's far too dangerous.'

Nina looked at him with liquid eyes. She opened her mouth to say something, changed her mind and buried her face into his chest again. Kamal felt her tears through his thin shirt.

—⁓—

Kamal opened the door. His brother Jalal stood in his jeans, a T-shirt with 'New York' printed across it and his Tom Jones hairstyle.

'Thought I'd drop by to visit Mamman,' Jalal said. The brothers kissed each other's faces.

'Mamman is visiting Mahin upstairs,' Kamal said as he led his brother to the kitchen. 'I've just brewed some tea. Stay and have some... or would you prefer something stronger?'

A devout Muslim even before the revolution, Jalal never missed his prayers or his fasting during the month of Ramadan. At funerals he sang the Koran rather than merely reciting it, closing his eyes and clipping a finger behind his ear as if listening for the praise of Allah. However, during the last three years he had started drinking alcohol.

'I heard about your episode with the brewed beer,' Jalal said laughingly. 'I think I'll stick to tea for now.'

Kamal poured two teas and took a seat across the table from his brother. He asked Jalal about his wife and daughters, but Jalal could tell his brother was not very interested in the answers he was giving.

'What's on your mind, Kamal? Is there something you wish to talk to me about?'

Kamal looked into his brother's face as if trying to make up his mind about something. He puffed air out of his cheeks. 'I need your help. But you have to first promise you will not utter any of this to anyone.'

Jalal pressed his brother's hand, 'You have my word.'

'We're leaving Iran,' Kamal said after a pause.

Jalal paled. 'You can't. You're on a stop list.'

'I know. I've found someone who will take us over the mountains to Turkey.'

'Kamal, this is madness.'

'I have no other choice. I cannot live here any longer.'

'Listen to me. Those roads are not safe,' Jalal reasoned. 'Everyday there are reports about travellers being ambushed by bandits. They'll kill you just for the shirts on your back. For God's sake just think about it.'

'I have thought about it,' Kamal slammed his fist down on the table. 'I think about it all the time. I also think about my nine-year-old son losing hair because he's traumatised. And I think about my twelve-year-old daughter being called a whore for not wearing a proper hejab. I think about the Komiteh Nina and I are regularly dragged to and interrogated by. I think about my friend's seventeen-year-old son with fifty lashes on his back. I think about all of them.'

As if wearied by his emotions, Kamal leaned back on his chair and closed his eyes. His head throbbed. He pressed his temples. 'They're killing us slowly anyway,' he continued in a softer voice. He lifted his eyes and looked into his brother's ashen face.

'At least this way there's a chance for a new life. Somewhere where the press is not censored and where my children could have the future I have dreamt for them.'

They sat in silence for awhile, each deep in their own thoughts.

'Have you told Mamman?' Jalal asked at last.

'No, aside from my business partners, and now you, no one else knows.'

Jalal straightened in his chair. His face assumed an expression of authority. 'Okay, since you have decided to go, we've got to think of a way to somehow trace your movements should we fail to hear from you. Tell me what you know about these people.'

Kamal shrugged his shoulders. 'I know very little about Haales. Except he's Turkish and he smuggles people for a living. However...there's one other thing,' Kamal hesitated, 'I think he might have an Iranian wife.'

Jalal's face brightened. 'That's great. We can put a tail on him,' he said. 'Find out where he lives. That way if we don't hear from you we can go back to his house.'

'How do we do that?' Kamal asked.

Jalal hesitated, 'We have to bring in Nasser.'

Nasser, Kamal's youngest brother, lived with his wife and baby in a one-bedroom apartment in the southern suburbs of Tehran. He had been thrown out of the university in their hometown of Tabriz a year ago for his communist beliefs. Since then he made a modest living working as a courier with his white Nissan truck.

The three men sat cross-legged across from one another in Nasser's apartment. The room was small with white-washed walls. In some of the corners the paint had started to chip. A naked bulb hung in the middle of the ceiling. The room was barely furnished, there were just a few cushions, two rolled-up mattresses in the corner, a sitar propped against the wall and an old faded Persian carpet.

Nasser had refused repeated offers of financial help from his brothers. He thanked them graciously as he handed back their envelopes of cash, assuring them he already had all that he needed.

'*Daddash*,' Nasser said in a hoarse voice, 'I can't believe what you're saying to me.' Tears streamed down his face. 'Since Baba died, you've been like a father to me. And now that you need my help, I'll do anything you ask. But I can't believe you're leaving.'

Kamal felt a tightness in his chest at the sight of his brother's tears.

'I'm meeting Haales tomorrow to tell him when I'll have his money ready,' Kamal explained. 'If I walk out of the coffee shop with him, I'll run a hand through my hair. I want you to follow him and tell me where he goes.'

Nasser called the following night.

'What did you find out?' asked Kamal, his fingers tightening around the receiver.

Nasser hesitated, 'Is it safe to speak over the phone?'

'Don't use any names. Did you find out where he lives?'

'Yes. And you're right. He does have an Iranian wife,' Nasser paused. 'Daddash, would these people be trustworthy . . . I mean with Nina and the kids?'

Kamal pressed his eyes shut. 'Only time will tell.'

I don't want to go...

At the same time England was celebrating the end of the Falklands War and the birth of Prince William, Dad announced that we were taking a trip in the next few weeks to the warm waters of Sarayin in the northwest of Iran.

'Why are we going there?' I asked. We rarely ventured far from the areas most frequented by the upper class, and never to villages.

'Your mother has been going to physio for some time now. Her doctor recommended she goes there.'

'I don't want to go,' I moaned. 'Why can't we go to the Caspian Sea like we always do?'

Dad ignored me.

'Why don't you stay at Tabriz and make day trips to the waters?' said Mamman. 'That way I can come with you. It will give me a chance to catch up with my brothers and sister and —'

'No,' Dad cut Mamman off. 'We're going with Jalal and we won't have any more room in the car. You have to stay with Mahin and Salman.'

The room fell silent. Dad had never spoken so forcefully to Mamman before. She squared her jaw and, without saying another word, left the room.

'I think this is the dumbest idea you've ever had,' I said unhappily, 'I want to stay back. You and Mum can go and you can take Mamman as well. That way everyone will be happy.'

'We are a family and we will go as a family,' Dad's voice sounded tired.

'Why?' I persisted.

'Because WE. ARE. A. FAMILY!' he shouted.

For the past few months, as part of his plan to get fit, Kamal had been going mountain-trekking every Friday. Walking in the foothills of the Alborz mountains was a popular pastime for the city's residents. About ten kilometres up the mountain was a restaurant where people could buy tea, sweets, barbecue chestnuts and lamb skewers cooked over hot charcoals and look out over Tehran covered in a blanket of smog. A double chair-lift took those who didn't wish to climb all the way from the foot of the mountain. Dad left at 4 am and walked fifteen kilometres up the mountain and back. He usually went alone and returned around 9 am. One morning, as he drove into the driveway, he saw Salman watering the garden.

'*Salaam*. May you be forever young!' Salman greeted Kamal jovially. 'Did you enjoy your trek?'

'The mountains are wonderful at this time of the morning.' Kamal looked out to the mountain with unfocused eyes. I'm really going to miss them, he thought.

'Salman, I need to talk to you,' Kamal said, moving closer to his brother-in-law. 'You know how Mamman is staying with you while we are away?'

'Of course. I don't want you to worry about it. Our home is her home,' Salman said without taking his eyes off his watering.

'I'm glad to hear it,' Kamal paused, wondering how to phrase his next sentence.

Salman, sensing a discomfort in Kamal, turned off the water and faced him. 'What's wrong, Kamal?'

Kamal pressed his fingers into his temple. He swallowed hard. 'We're not going to the warm waters.' He grabbed Salman's arm and pulled him closer. 'We're escaping through the mountains to Turkey,' he whispered into his ear.

Salman paled. 'I...I...don't understand,' he stammered.

'We didn't want to tell anybody. Aside from my partners and my brothers, you are the only other person I've told. We don't think it's safe to tell too many people. I am telling you because I need your help.'

Kamal paused, measuring his words. 'I need a place for Mamman to stay...for good.'

Salman nodded. 'She can stay with us. Our home is her home.'

'Another thing, you can't tell anyone, not even Mahin, what we just talked about. Not until you hear from us again.'

'When will that be?'

'Hopefully within a few days,' Kamal answered, '. . . from Turkey.'

'Kamal, I have to tell my mother,' Mum pleaded in hushed voice.

We were in the car, driving to Eshrat Mamman's house for a family dinner before we left on our trip the next day.

'Nina, we've talked about this,' Dad reasoned.

'I have to,' Mum persisted.

Dad looked at her with an expression of sympathy and love.

'I can't go without telling her,' she said with a shaky voice.

'Tell her what?' I asked, leaning forward from the backseat.

'Never mind,' they both said in unison.

We drove in silence. The city still wore her black veil each night and the streets were almost deserted. We passed several Komiteh barricades. Dad slowed down as we passed each one, careful not to draw attention to us. Young men in army greens and machine guns across their backs directed traffic.

The sky was blue–black. From the window I could see the moon entangled in the trees. Ever since the blackouts the stars and the moon seemed a lot brighter, but they still had to fight through the thick smog.

'The moon is a half–crescent tonight,' I said. 'A few more nights and there will be a full moon.'

At Eshrat Mamman's house there was a flurry of activity. The women had all congregated in the kitchen. The air was thick with steam and the aroma of spices. I loved watching the women as they prepared the dishes and caught up on gossip.

But tonight Mum was unusually quiet. She kept looking over her shoulder at her mother.

When it came to serving the food, I was starting to get in everyone's way. 'Come with me child,' Aziz gently pulled me away.

Aziz was my great-grandmother. She had long white hair to her waist which she combed and braided every morning. Her touch was gentle and her voice soothing. She stringed necklaces for me with jasmine flowers while telling me stories.

'There! How pretty you look with your new necklace. And the sweet aroma of jasmine is bound to drive all the angels in heaven drunk with delight.'

I hugged her.

'Dinner!' Eshrat Mamman called out and we all gathered around the big dining table.

During dinner the conversation changed to the exodus of Iranians through the Pakistan and Turkey borders.

'It's not just young men,' Mahmood was saying. 'It's men, women, kids, grandparents. Some of these people get ambushed by bandits before they even get to the border,' he shook his head. 'Some are abandoned by smugglers if they don't give them more money. The stories are everywhere around the borders and yet every week hundreds try to cross.'

Mum and Dad were unusually quiet. Eshrat Mamman got up and started to collect the dishes. Mum quickly got up too.

'I don't know why these people don't try to cope like the rest of us,' Eshrat Mamman said. 'They are crazy risking their lives like that.'

Mum and Dad exchanged a look. Mum's skin looked thin and stretched across her face. 'Don't get up,' she told her sisters when they rose from their chairs. 'Mamman and I can manage.'

It took a long time before the two women finally emerged from the kitchen with trays of tea. Eshrat Mamman was wiping her eyes with a tissue and Mum was trying to soothe her. When asked by others what had happened, Mum said onion had got into Eshrat Mamman's eyes. Everyone could tell Mum was lying, especially as she was not very good at it, but they did not press the issue.

We left straight after tea in order to be home before the curfew. Outside, Mum and Eshrat Mamman held one another for a long time. Their shoulders shook as they tried to stifle their crying. Eshrat Mamman then held Behzad and me, rocking us in her arms. She pressed her wet face against us while repeating, 'God, I give my children to your keeping.'

I couldn't understand why she was so upset. 'Mum drags her leg a little and her doctor recommended the warm waters,' I offered. 'Don't worry, Mamman. Mum's leg will get better and we'll be back soon.'

Eshrat Mamman sank on the bottom stair and stroked my face. There were fresh tears in her eyes. She opened and closed her mouth as if to say something. Instead she buried her face in her hands and wept.

'Take them, Kamal. I don't want them to see me like this.' She wiped her face with the back of her sleeve. 'Go. My prayers are with you.'

Mum cried the whole way home.

The Escape

Tabriz

Nina checked the contents of the bag against her list. A change of clothes and underwear — check. Pyjamas and hairbrushes — check. Toothbrushes, toothpaste, cleanser, moisturiser, shaving cream — check. As an afterthought she added the shampoo.

She checked the stitching of the bag. The previous night Jalal had sewn US dollars into the seams. The bag looked bulky in parts, but unless someone was looking thoroughly it was not obvious.

Her bed was made. Her dressing-gown was folded neatly at its foot. Her make-up and perfumes were lined on her dresser just like any other day. After breakfast she had washed the dishes and put the feta and butter back into the fridge.

'It's as if it's just an ordinary day,' she whispered to herself. An image of her mother flashed before her eyes and her chest tightened. She felt hot tears behind her eyes. There was a soft knock on the door.

'Nina.' Kamal's face peered through, 'It's time to go.'

He was wearing the new leather shoes she had bought him at *NoRuz*. He smiled a little shyly when he noticed her looking at them. 'I thought I'd need a good pair of shoes when we get to Australia.'

She smiled weakly then rose to join him. The kids were waiting in the living room on the grey sofa. Nina walked around the apartment. Her eyes focusing on every single item, etching them into her memory.

Every piece of furniture, bedding, painting, rug, kitchenware, chinaware, jewellery, toys and books had been catalogued and a price set on it. In less than two weeks the Persian rugs would be rolled up against the wall. Relatives, neighbours and strangers would be all over her apartment. The women's heels clicking on the Italian tiles with their husbands reluctantly in tow as they handled the ornaments and crystals she had collected on her travels; fighting for the more original pieces, and haggling over the price. She was glad she would not be there to see it.

'Nina,' Kamal said, bringing her back from her daydream, 'I've got the holy Koran.'

She held the Koran over the door as Kamal passed under it and out the door, back and out the door again, a ceremony to ensure a safe journey. After everyone had passed through, Nina held the Koran and pressed her lips and forehead against it. Her fingers trembled slightly as she closed the door, hearing the lock click behind her for the last time.

—⚭—

Downstairs, our aunts and uncles were waiting to see us off. Dad pressed his sisters to himself, holding them a little longer than usual. He shook the men's hands warmly. Mum was more subdued. She kissed and shook hands with few words and glassy eyes.

Despite my protests, I was beginning to get excited about our trip. In my arms I was carrying my walkman with my *Grease* tape and a hardcover copy of *Gone with the Wind* that I was reading for the second time. I waved excitedly as we pulled out of the driveway and couldn't work out why Mum was so quiet. My aunts splashed water on the car as we drove off to ensure a safe return.

Tabriz is 600 kilometres northwest of Tehran. The sun was descending behind an amber horizon by the time we arrived. The roads had been packed with travellers in overcrowded cars escaping the heat of Tehran and heading to the cooler climate of Azarbaijan, or visiting family in other parts of the country. We'd made a few short stops for lunch, to stretch our legs, and to change drivers. It was July 1982 and we were travelling in the holy month of Ramadan. Uncle Jalal, who was also travelling with us, was fasting and didn't eat during the day. The rest of us had lunched in the car on bread and grapes Mum had brought, careful not to be seen by other travellers. If the Komiteh guard caught us eating during Ramadan they would take us to the local headquarters and we'd be at the mercy of the local cleric's ruling.

Dad's family had grown up in Tabriz and only spoke Turkish until they'd moved to Tehran when Dad was seventeen. Now, Dad and Jalal spoke in Turkish as they tried to find a particular address in the winding streets of their old hometown. We finally stopped in front of a motel with graffitied walls and a rusted 'Motel Asia' sign hanging above its entry. The building had long lost its colour and turned grey. Outside, the Koran was being recited from a loudspeaker to streets packed with vendors and women in black chadors doing their last-minute shopping. Dad and Jalal got out of the car and went inside the motel.

'Dad's not serious about getting a room here is he?' I asked, sticking my head out the window to get a better look at the building. As a child I had always been intrigued by the stories Dad told us from his childhood in Tabriz and the look of longing that would pass over his eyes as he spoke. I could see my father and Uncle Jalal as young boys, darting through the ancient streets, chasing one another in play. The clipped painted walls of the motel didn't match my image of Tabriz and I couldn't help the disappointment that descended in my heart.

An old man with a tuft of white hair sat on a low chair behind the counter. He sat so stooped his head was barely visible.

'Yes,' he pulled himself slowly to his feet, scratching his three-day growth.

'I need a room for a family,' said Kamal.

'Don't have any.' He was about to sink back into his seat when he spotted a man in a peasant outfit carrying live chickens.

'*Baradar*! Where are you going with those? This is a motel not a zoo.'

'I've come to sell my chickens, *pedar*,' the man said, calling him 'father' as a mark of respect for his old age.

'Outside, *baradar*. Sell them outside.'

During the exchange Kamal had reached into his pocket and laid some money on the counter.

'No, *baradar*,' the old man waved the money away. 'I don't have any room. Come back tomorrow when some more of the travellers have gone.'

Kamal's back tensed. Haales had said he would meet them here tomorrow and they had no way of contacting him.

'They say they have no room,' Dad said with his head through the window.

Mum paled. 'What are we going to do?'

'Before anything else, we'd better get a room somewhere,' Uncle Jalal offered, 'we don't want to be out when martial law starts.'

We got a room at the international hotel. It was built in the European style, with European bathrooms. The interiors were neatly kept and the rooms were spacious. Our window looked out onto a well-maintained pool. The late afternoon light danced on the water's surface. The pool was so inviting and yet unattainable. Two women in full Islamic uniform lazed on the deck chairs with their heads close to one another. One of them said something and they both laughed.

'Summer Nights' blared though my walkman as I watched the women by the pool. Dad paced the room with his fingers pressing his temples. He suddenly stopped and snapped his fingers.

'Of course! Haales said he'd be flying here. We'll go to the airport in the morning and wait for him. Then we can tell him where we are staying.'

His mood changed after that and he ordered some kebabs and barbecued corn cobs for dinner. We spent the remainder of the evening driving around Tabriz. The parks were packed with happy families breaking their fast with a picnic while their children splashed around the water fountains. The blackened city lights had not dampened people's spirits. Everywhere people shared their meals and talked loudly over one another under the dim light of the moon. Dad told us how as a teenage boy he would walk around the same fountain with his friends hoping to catch the eyes of local girls. He used to scribble Hafez poetry on pieces of paper which he secretly passed into their hands as they walked past. Dad and Uncle Jalal talked in nostalgic voices as they recalled their childhood. It wasn't long before martial law forced us back to our hotel. I slept solidly that night, exhausted from the long day of travelling.

Haales had told Kamal that he was flying to Tabriz. There were only two scheduled flights from Tehran to Tabriz and the first flight was due to land in twenty minutes.

The airport was small and crowded. The fluorescent lights made a slight buzzing sound which seemed to grow louder the longer Kamal waited. The air felt stifled with so many people crowded in a small space. The few hard bench seats in the waiting area were occupied with families. Mothers held their chadors between their teeth while keeping a tight grip on their baggage and toddlers.

Kamal searched the crowd anxiously in case Haales had already arrived on another flight.

'Let's wait outside,' Jalal pulled at his brother's sleeve. They spread their coats on a grassy hill with others. From where they sat they could see the front gate clearly. They watched a plane land.

'I'll stay here, Kamal. It might spook them if they see me with you,' Jalal said.

Kamal waited at the arrival area. He scanned every face. As the crowd thinned out, his chest tightened. He swallowed hard. He waited long after the last passenger had gone before walking back outside.

'He wasn't on the plane,' Kamal said in a tight voice. Images of Haales being caught kept flashing through his head.

Jalal placed a hand on his brother's shoulder and squeezed it. 'The next is in four hours. He'll most likely be on that one.'

Kamal nodded, distracted by dark thoughts.

It was late in the afternoon when the second flight from Tehran landed. Kamal and Jalal had not eaten or drunk anything all day. Kamal's lips were dry and his throat was parched.

The travellers looked expectantly amongst the waiting crowd, dragging their heavy suitcases and bundles behind them. People waiting called out and waved.

'Ali Jan . . . Over here . . . Ali!'

'Geeta . . .'

'Golam . . .'

'Mohammad . . .'

On hearing their names, the travellers dropped their bags to embrace their families, forming islands of weeping blackclad women and unshaven men.

Kamal continued to scan the faces. A few times he thought he saw Haales, but it turned out to be another man. The fluorescent lights above him started to blink, buzzing louder with every passing minute.

Outside again, Kamal sank heavily next to Jalal and buried his head in his hands. 'We got scammed. He's taken our money and screwed us.' His head felt like shattered glass. 'I failed my family. What am I going to say to Nina?'

'You'll say nothing yet. First we're going to call Nasser,' Jalal said.

Kamal looked at him, puzzled.

'He knows where Haales's house is,' Jalal said, 'we'll ask him to pay a visit.'

Two hours later Kamal dialled his brother's number again.

'Allo,' Nasser's voice crackled through the phone.

'Nasser, it's me.' It was a bad connection and Kamal had to speak loudly into the mouthpiece. 'Did you speak to our friend?'

'No. He wasn't there. I spoke to his wife. She nearly fainted when she saw me.'

Good, thought Kamal. 'What did she say?' he tightened his grip on the receiver.

'She swore they had missed the flight and were travelling up by car. She said they will be there tomorrow.'

Kamal's grip relaxed. 'Thanks. I appreciate everything you've done for us these past few months.'

'Daddash,' Nasser paused. 'I love you,' his voice filled with concern.

'I love you too,' Kamal said, feeling a flood of tenderness towards his younger brother. 'We'll call you as soon as we can.' He hung up quickly.

He turned to Jalal, 'They'll be here tomorrow,' and felt relief wash over him.

The visitor

That evening Uncle Jalal drove us to Motel Asia.

'What are we doing back here again?' I said in disbelief.

Dad and Uncle Jalal were unpacking our bags from the back and Mum and Behzad were already out of the car.

'You're not serious, are you?' I asked, searching their faces.

'It's only for a night,' Dad said in a voice that did not invite any arguments.

'What was wrong with our last hotel?' I asked, not giving in.

'Nothing, we just want to stay here tonight.'

'Daddy?' Forgetting my promise to call him Baba and trying hard to fight back the tears. 'I never knew you were so cheap!'

I stormed past them and leaned against the entry with folded arms, my eyebrows in a tight knit.

Uncle Jalal said he would be leaving that morning. He had to visit a police station to help them with an investigation on a case.

'How will we get back home?' I asked.

Dad and Uncle Jalal exchanged a look. 'I have hired a driver to take us to the warm waters,' Dad said. 'When we get back, we'll catch a plane home.'

I thought this was a little strange, but Dad's demeanour didn't encourage any more questions. He looked agitated and his answers to my questions were clipped and carried a hint of annoyance. Mum stroked his back and murmured in his ears. But her soothing touch was not enough to ease his tension.

Mum and Dad embraced Uncle Jalal warmly, thanking him repeatedly. He hugged Behzad and me, smiling at us with soft eyes. His expression reminded me of a father on his daughter's wedding day. A mixture of pride and sadness in seeing his child go. I showed little emotion, partly blaming him for the move.

Upstairs, I flung myself on the bed and cried. I was angry with my parents. I was upset for being dragged on such a horrible holiday and having to stay in a dirty room that stank of cheap cigarettes and unwashed bodies.

Mum and Dad largely ignored me. Behzad zoomed his matchbox car around the bed, occasionally looking up at me with concern. I stopped crying after awhile and sat up in bed. Through the thin walls I could hear a mother screaming at her children. Mum was on the double bed with her feet tucked under her. Behzad leaned on her, his eyes heavy with sleep. She was telling him a story I had heard several times. It was the one about the goat, her three kids and a big bad wolf. As a child it was my favourite story, I made my grandmother repeat it to me over and over. Dad was in the shower. The pipes rattled every time he turned the tap on.

Outside, the sky was slowly changing colour from peach to grey. The moon was almost a full circle and sat high in the sky. The mosque's loudspeaker called the faithful to their evening prayer and the end of their fast for the day.

I switched on my bedside lamp. It didn't work. I clicked at the switch several times. Nothing. I blew air through clenched teeth. I took my copy of *Gone with the Wind* and moved a chair to the middle of the room where the main light shined brightest, and immersed myself in Scarlett and her battles. The Civil War, Tara, Ashley and Rhett helped to block out the rattling pipes and the loudspeakers.

I didn't even look up when there was a knock on the door. At first Mum didn't move. A few seconds later the knock came again. This time Mum shifted the sleeping Behzad off her and placed his head gently on the pillow. She covered him, pulled a scarf over her head and went to the door. I could see her talking to someone through a slit in the door. The stranger had a deep, soft voice. I heard him say our surname.

'Wait here,' Mum told him, closed the door, then quickly went into the bathroom.

She spoke to Dad in hushed tones. A moment later Dad came out in jeans, a fresh shirt and bare feet.

'How does he know my name?' he asked.

'I don't know...I...I...didn't ask,' Mum stammered.

Dad opened the door and went out. A few minutes later he came back in and went straight for his shoes and coat. 'I have to go out for awhile. I'll be back soon.'

'Who is he? What does he want? Where are you going?' Mum followed Dad to the door, dragging her leg a little. 'It's

going to be martial law shortly,' she said, her voice trembling
at the words.

Dad checked his watch. 'I still have time. I'll be back before
martial law at 10.30.'

'What's your name?' Kamal asked the stranger as they descended
the steps two at a time

'Behrooz. I have been waiting all day outside the motel for
Haales. But he never showed up. In desperation I called Haj
Ali and he gave me your name.' Behrooz was breathing hard
as he tried to keep up with Kamal.

Outside, the streets were dark. All the streetlamps and
windows had been darkened because of the war.

Kamal narrowed his eyes. 'How come he gave you my name?
Why didn't you get a room of your own?'

'I don't have any identification. I gave it to Haales. No one
will give me a room without it,' Behrooz's voice was almost
pleading. 'They'll throw me in jail if they catch me in the
streets without any identification during martial law. I have a
young wife. I . . .' his voice trailed off.

Kamal stopped to take a better look at Behrooz. He wasn't
sure yet if he could trust him. In his mid-thirties, Behrooz
was of medium build with a receding hairline. His complexion
was fair with rosy cheeks which had turned redder from running.
He had round gentle eyes. He looked scared.

'Okay, now listen up. I have an uncle who lives not far from
here. You can stay there.' Kamal checked his watch, 'We'd
better hurry.'

He started to run down the street towards the bazaar with Behrooz close behind. Past the bazaars, they came to a part of Tabriz where the houses were built in a haphazard order and the narrow streets snaked around mud houses. Kamal had not been in these parts since he was seventeen and he was surprised by how narrow the streets were where he had once played. His shoes pinched. He cursed himself for not bringing his joggers. Once in a while he stopped at a mud house which looked familiar, but he couldn't be sure. The sky had turned black. There were no streetlights. The only light was from the moon.

Kamal stopped. 'I can't find it,' he said, breathing hard. He checked his watch. 8.45 pm. He cursed under his breath. He looked up and down the street and found what he was looking for. 'I have to make a phonecall.'

'Allo,' Nasser's voice filled the receiver.

'It's me, Kamal. I have another problem. It's one of my employees.' He didn't feel he needed to tell Nasser the truth. The less Nasser was involved the better. 'The office told him where to find me. The idiot has forgotten to bring his identification papers on an audit. No hotel will give him a room. Do you know anyone from your university days here who will put him up for the night?'

The taxi did not look like it was going to stop. Two had already passed them. Kamal stepped off the curve, waving his arms wildly. The address Nasser had given him was for the apartment blocks close to the hospital. The taxi pulled over. There were already three passengers in the car. Kamal checked his watch: 9.00 pm. Only ninety minutes before martial law.

'Where are you going?' the driver asked.

Kamal pushed Behrooz in and squeezed in after him.

'*Baradar*, I'm desperate!' Kamal said in Turkish. 'I've just found out my child has been hit by a car.'

The other passengers clucked their tongues and shook their heads in sympathy. A woman in the backseat bit down on her lip, beat her chest with an open palm and muttered a prayer under her breath. Next to her, Behrooz sat stupefied, not understanding the conversation going on around him.

'God is merciful,' the driver said, 'where is your child now?'

'They took him to hospital. *Inshallah*, we will not be too late,' Kamal said to the other passengers. The driver and other passengers agreed that Kamal and Behrooz should be dropped off first. Fifteen minutes later the taxi pulled up in front of the hospital. Kamal gave the driver a big tip.

'I have prayed for your child,' the woman in the backseat said.

'Thank you, sister,' Kamal said, feeling a little guilty for having lied.

As soon as the taxi left, Kamal and Behrooz started to run in the direction Nasser had given. They found the apartment and knocked on the door. No one answered. Panic rose inside Kamal. He knocked louder.

'Who is it?' A man's frightened voice asked from the other side of the door.

'Reza? I'm Kamal Dastyari, Nasser's brother.'

They heard the click of the lock and the door opened. Reza stood pale in a white T-shirt and pyjama pants.

'*Salaam*, Agha Dastyari,' he said respectfully and stood aside to let the two men in. 'Please excuse my attire, but I was not expecting company. When you knocked I thought you might be ... well, you know the government is not sympathetic towards those with socialist ideals.' Reza offered his guests the only two chairs in the room, insisting he was more comfortable sitting on the floor.

'Could I get you any tea or a glass of Pepsi?' He was confused as to the purpose of the men's visit but did not consider it polite to ask.

'No, I will not trouble you any more than I have to.' Kamal switched to Turkish. 'What can I say?' He threw his hands in the air. 'It's my stupid employee here.' Pointing to Behrooz who looked back with wide eyes, 'God knows I'm going to sack him as soon as I get back to Tehran. The idiot has got us both in a fix.'

'What has he done?' Reza's eyes moved from one man's face to another.

'Don't worry he doesn't speak Turkish,' Kamal said, waving a dismissive hand in Behrooz's direction. 'And to make matters worse, he's forgotten to bring his papers.'

'How can I help?' Reza offered.

'We just need a place for him to stay tonight.'

'But ...'

'Nasser spoke highly of you. He said you will not leave us out in the streets.'

'Yes ... of course,' Reza said a little hesitantly.

'Well, that settles it.' Kamal rose quickly to his feet before Reza could object. 'I must be off.' He shook hands with both men and told Behrooz to meet him at his motel room in the morning. As he was leaving, Kamal checked his watch. 10.15 pm. There wasn't much time left. ·

He started running.

Nina paced the room. She sat down when her leg began to ache. After months of physio, it was still not fully healed. She checked her watch: 10.40.

Martial law had started ten minutes ago and Kamal was not back yet. She wanted a cigarette but since a few months ago, when she had fallen ill from asthma, she had not been able to smoke.

The curtains were drawn and the only light in the room was from the slit under the door. She continued to pace.

Nina froze when she saw a shadow move behind the door. Someone turned the latch. The door opened, flooding the small room with a soft light. Kamal stood there, looking tired. She ran to him, throwing her arms around his neck.

'I thought they had caught you. I didn't know what I'd do if...' her shoulders shook. She buried her head in his neck and wept. Kamal stroked her back. He was breathing hard and his feet ached.

'It will be okay,' he said, not convinced if he believed it himself.

Behrooz arrived early the next morning. Dad introduced him as a colleague who would be spending the day with us.

Dad and Behrooz played cards with a deck Behrooz had brought with him. They were both in good humour, teasing one another as to who was the best player. Once in awhile Dad checked his watch and frowned.

'Should we call?' Behrooz asked.

'His wife said they'll be here. We'll call if they don't show by three.'

The loud knock on the door came in the mid-afternoon, startling Mum and Behzad who were curled up on the bed. Mum sat up straight and stared wildly at the door. Dad opened it to let in a slight man with a trimmed moustache. They shook hands and spoke in Turkish. The man looked excited. He paced around the room speaking rapidly. Dad looked as if he had trouble following what was being said. He offered the man a seat. The man hesitated then sat down, placing a cigarette between his lips. He lit it, masking his face behind a cloud of smoke. He was silent for awhile. I found myself fascinated by how quickly his knee jerked up and down. He noticed me staring and stopped. Mum and Dad shared a look but remained silent.

The man suddenly stood, stabbed his cigarette in the ashtray and pulled out two bundles, handing them to Dad and Behrooz. It was money and passports wrapped in strings.

'What are you doing?' At full height Dad was an inch taller than the other man.

'You have to keep these,' the man spoke Farsi in a thick accent. 'It's become too dangerous for me to keep them.'

'But you were supposed to carry them for us,' Dad spat his words out.

'Please, take now,' the man insisted.

Behrooz looked nervously at Dad who remained motionless. The man's eyes darkened. He knocked over the chair he had been sitting on, knelt beside it and pulled a switch knife out of his pocket. I heard Mum drew in a breath as her hand clasped over her mouth.

'Haales, what are —' Before Dad could finish his sentence, Haales had slit the mattress, sticking the bundles of cash in the gap. He then quickly stood up facing Dad and Behrooz. 'The driver will be here at four. Be ready!'

For the next two hours Mum and Dad checked and re-checked our bag. They seemed to pay careful attention to the seams. They had disagreed a little over where they should hide the passports but decided they didn't have much time so Dad hid them down his pants.

My few queries about who the man was and where we were going went largely unanswered. I had become curiously used to the silence, the nervous exchanges, the hushed tones, and meetings with men introduced as Dad's colleagues, and so I queried them less and less.

Mum and I were dressed in our Islamic uniform. Mum took special care in making sure there were no loose strands of hair sticking out.

Behrooz played nervously with his moustache. He had no bags, just a toothbrush which he carried in his lightweight jacket.

Time to go

The knock on the door was gentle, almost inaudible. Mum and Dad exchanged a look. Mum smiled reassuringly back at Dad and pulled Behzad and I closer to her, placing a gentle kiss on our foreheads.

Dad went to the door, opening it just wide enough to stick his head through. He spoke to a man on the other side in hushed tones. He closed the door and turned to face us.

'Time to go,' he said with a nervous smile.

Dad picked up our bag, grabbed Behzad's hand, and noiselessly walked out, followed by Mum, Behrooz and me. Nobody spoke as we descended the stairs. On the ground floor, instead of taking us through the foyer, Dad led us out a smaller back door that opened to a narrow alley. The afternoon sun had disappeared behind dark clouds.

A brown Peykan, an Iranian-manufactured car, with mud stains all over its wheels and lower bonnet was parked ten metres away. A man in faded Levis and a white shirt with rolled-up sleeves motioned us to come over. Dad quickened his step, forcing the rest of us to run to keep up with him.

A pungent smell of cheap cigarettes, sweat and fear greeted us as Mum, Behrooz and I climbed in the back of the car. Dad and Behzad shared the front passenger seat. The seats were vinyl and chipped in places, sticking into us when we sat on them. Worry beads hung from the rearview mirror and a picture of Imam Ali was stuck next to one of Khomeini on the windscreen.

The engine roared into life. The gravel crunched and ricocheted off the car as the driver pressed hard on the accelerator. He lit a cigarette and offered one to Dad who refused. Mum coughed in the backseat and rolled down the window to let in some air. The driver drove at a terrifying speed, cutting in-between traffic. He had one hand resting on the car horn, which he used liberally, all the time muttering to himself. It was late afternoon and there was not much traffic on the road. In a few short hours people would pour out of their homes heading to one of the few parks to break their fast around a picnic spread. Dad gripped Behzad with one hand and held tight against the door handle with the other.

Kamal watched the speedometer. It only went to 160 km/h and the driver was pressing 100.

'Why don't you slow down?' he said in Turkish.

'I think we are being followed,' the driver said, throwing nervous glances at his rearview mirror.

Kamal tried to look through the side mirror. 'Are you sure?'

The driver nodded. 'The van behind us is a Komiteh van.'

Kamal twisted as far as he could to look behind him, but he couldn't see a van. Thunder clapped above, followed by a lightning flash. Heavy raindrops fell as the car took a sharp turn, heading out of Tabriz.

On the open road, outside the city limits the driver pressed harder on the accelerator. The speed dial shook unsteadily at 110 km/h. Thankfully there were very few cars on the road. Kamal stretched his neck to see if there were any vans behind, but all he could see were sheets of rain.

'I don't think we are being followed anymore,' he said to the driver. 'Why don't you slow down?' The wipers worked furiously through the pouring rain, making the driver squint. He was concentrating hard and did not seem to hear. Kamal again asked him to slow down.

'We are behind schedule,' the driver said, not taking his eyes off the road. 'We left too late and have to make up for lost time.'

Kamal turned to look at Nina. She suffered badly from carsickness and looked pale. She winced as the car went over a bump in the road. 'How's your leg?' he asked.

She smiled weakly. 'I'll be fine.'

At around 8 pm we stopped to eat at a small coffee house, where a few other cars were parked. The heavy rain had eased into a light shower and then finally stopped. We filed out of the car, all stiff, sweaty and queasy. I was thankful for the break. I was hungry, thirsty and badly in need of a toilet. Around the back we found a squat toilet. It was old but clean. A small window allowed natural light in during the day and there was a small watering can to wash ourselves with. I had never gotten used to squatting and had to hold on to the walls to balance myself. I wondered how Mum was going to manage with her bad leg. Outside the toilet I washed my hands with hard soap under a cold tap. My stomach grumbled from the smell of kebabs wafting through the air.

Inside the coffee house, the rest of our travelling party were seated on plastic chairs around a plastic table. The driver sat next to Dad, smoking and muttering to himself. He jumped at the sound of every approaching car, studying the faces of its occupants with suspicion.

The place was a mud house with white-washed walls that stood bare except for a framed picture of Khomeini. A young boy around my age, with thin limbs and a faded AC/DC T-shirt, served tea and wiped down the tables with a stained cloth. A man cooked skewers of lamb, chicken and tomatoes on hot coals, fanning the coals with a large piece of cardboard to keep them hot. Once ready, he served the food on lavash bread, sprinkling it with sumac.

It reminded me of my grandmother, hunched over her hot coals fanning them feverishly as the meat sizzled on the grill. I remembered the last dinner we had had there a few nights ago. How she pressed me against her, wetting my face with her tears. Suddenly my chest tightened and tears stung my eyes, threatening to overflow. I wanted to go back. Back home where things made sense and back to my grandmother.

In the car park, a military van pulled up, sloshing its heavy tyres through the mud. About a dozen young soldiers in their early twenties and dressed in army greens jumped out. They were in good humour, smiling and joking with one another.

Our driver stiffened as soon as he saw them. His left shoulder twitched and his mutterings became louder. I heard Dad whisper to Mum and Behrooz that the driver thought we had been spotted.

'He doesn't look very sane to me,' Mum whispered.

'I don't think we have much choice but to listen to what he says,' Dad said.

I wanted to stand up and shout at my parents. Yell at them at the top of my voice for dragging us here with this madman, with his death wish on the road and his insane mutterings. But I said nothing. Something in their pale expression and strained eyes told me to stay quiet. Instead I nodded when they asked me to eat my food quickly.

Back in the car, it didn't take long for the vinyl seat to stick to my jeans and my Islamic uniform, making my legs and back sweaty and clammy. In the front seat Behzad had fallen asleep with his head resting on Dad's chest.

We were driving very fast; so fast that the car shook. The driver kept checking his rearview mirror. He said things in Turkish to Dad, which made my father press at his temple and stretch his neck to look behind us.

We passed the sign for the turn off to Bazargon. I heard Dad whisper to Behrooz that Bazargan was the border town to Turkey. The driver did not slow down to turn. About a kilometre past the turn-off he suddenly turned onto a dirt road and switched off the car lights. It was pitch black with little moon to offer assistance. Dad shot a look at the driver in the dim light. The man seemed to be in his element. He had stopped muttering and his features were tense in concentration. His eyes hardly blinked as he focused on the dirt road, until the car stopped suddenly under an oak tree.

'Where are we?' Kamal asked as he tried to focus his eyes in the vast darkness. There was a noise, like the sound of twigs breaking, followed by heavy footsteps, running towards the car. He felt a chill run through his body as the doors flung open and two men in provincial clothes and rifles slung across their bodies squeezed in — one in the front with him and one in the back next to Behrooz. The two men could not close the car doors completely so held them closed with their hands, as the driver once again pressed on the accelerator.

The men were Kurds. They had weather-beaten skin and smelled of sweat and earth. The car bounced up and down, splattering mud inside.

Kamal's heart beat fast. He felt clammy and sick for bringing his family this far. His mind was racing. What if they attack us? Behrooz did not seem strong enough to help him fight them off. What were the guns for? What if they just shoot us and throw us into unmarked graves?

'What have I done?' he said under his breath. 'Dear God! What have I done?' Despite the cool air rushing through the partially open door, a string of sweat beads had gathered on his forehead.

The car stopped in a meadow with tall grass. The two Kurds got out and took out their torches. Everyone else remained in their seats.

'This is where you get off,' the driver said.

'Where is this place? Who are these men and where are they taking us?' Kamal asked.

'I don't know,' the driver said in a matter-of-fact tone. 'I've done my job. Get out.'

The two Kurdish men waited patiently outside. Nina reached over and pressed Kamal's shoulder. 'Kamal, I think we've come too far and have little choice but to put our trust in these people.' Kamal dropped his eyes and nodded. 'One other thing,' she paused. 'It's time the children knew.'

I sat with my body pressed against the car door. My heart pounded in my chest. Mum's words rang in my ears. What was it they were about to tell us? Dad climbed into the backseat next to me, avoiding my gaze as he did so. Everyone except the driver and us had climbed out of the car. The driver tapped his fingers on the dashboard and muttered to himself. Dad picked up my book from where it had fallen under the seat and gave it to me, slowly lifting his eyes to meet mine. The car door was open and a dim light flooded the inside.

'I have something to tell you.' Dad smiled nervously, not sure how to phrase his sentence. I pressed my book against my chest, shielding myself against what was to come.

'We are leaving Iran,' he said. I saw him opening and closing his lips around the four words but the sentence did not sink in. The whole world seemed to shrink around me and I shuddered.

'Leaving Iran?' I stared back at him, stupefied.

He took my trembling hand in his. 'These men are going to help us escape through the mountains to Turkey.' His words made me tremble with a coldness that made me feel like my body was free-falling through the air.

'You're scaring me, Daddy.' My voice was so weak it was barely audible to me.

I could see Mum's silhouette kneeling on the grass. She had Behzad's face cupped in her hands. Behrooz stood at a respectable distance, holding our bag with his head bowed.

'We need you to be strong,' Dad said.

I wanted to assure him that I was strong but the words froze in my throat, choking me like a large lump I couldn't swallow. I kept my eyes down so he couldn't see the hot tears that blurred my vision. I tried to blink them back but one escaped and rolled freely down my face. The image of my grandmother sitting on her porch flashed in my mind again, her arms wrapped around her knees, crying as her body rocked back and forth. She must have known. I wanted to run to her now, to bury my face in her lap, and feel her arms envelop me. She knew she wasn't going to see us again and yet she had let us go.

Dad gently lifted my chin and wiped away my tear. His own eyes were moist. 'In a few days we'll be in Australia,' he said.

Why Australia? I thought. Nobody goes to Australia. I fought hard to try to remember anything I could about Australia. Then I remembered Dad's friend we had gone to visit. Didn't Mum say he was Australian? I wondered if he was the reason we were going there. I also remembered an article my cousin Zoya had translated for me from a French magazine. It was about Olivia Newton-John, another Australian.

The driver said something to Dad in Turkish.

'We have to go now,' he said, 'are you ready?'

I smiled weakly and nodded.

As I was getting out I left my book on the backseat. I ran my fingers along its hard cover and through its well-read pages. It was the first part of two volumes. The second part sat on my bookshelf. What would happen to it? 'I can't take you where I'm going,' I said and closed the car door behind me.

Outside the car, I saw Dad pull his Swiss Army knife out of our bag and slip it into his jeans.

Starless sky

The starless sky offered little in the way of light. The moon
was no more than a thin wafer behind the clouds. For the last
thirty minutes, my ears had become tuned to the sound of the
tap-tapping of footsteps on muddy roads. I had learned to
distinguish between the heavy footsteps of our guides — one
leading, and the other bringing up the rear — the light steps
of Behzad, and the slight drag of Mum's right leg.

We passed through a few villages. Every village had dogs to
protect against intruders. The dogs did not belong to any
particular household and roamed freely between the mud
houses. They would start barking as soon as they picked up
our scents. The guides made us run through the villages,
throwing rocks at the dogs to keep them away when they got
too close. We could clearly see their white teeth glistening and
hear the growl in their throats.

My heart pounded as we ran past a small cluster of houses. A warm glow shone from behind the heavy rugs draped over the windows. Inside the hut, a family would be sitting down to dinner. The head of the household would strain his ears when the dogs started barking and would hear the sound of running feet. He would exchange a knowing look with his wife. These were familiar sounds to them now and he no longer pulled back the rug to take a look.

We came to a ditch. A small stream snaked through it.

'Agha Dastyari, *salaam*,' a man's voice called out.

We froze. Somebody there knew our name and was expecting us. I was holding Mum's hand and her fingers stiffened around mine. Dad searched the darkness in the direction the voice came from. His eyes were wide with confusion.

'I trust your journey has not been too difficult,' the man's voice came again.

My breath became shallow as my heart pounded harder against my shirt. I looked around for the guides but they had dissolved into the night.

Kamal's heart had skipped a beat when he heard his name from across the ditch. The voice sounded familiar but he couldn't recall where from. Then he remembered.

'Is that you, Hassan?' he said, barely able to contain his excitement.

'Yes, Agha. Welcome.' A shadow emerged from the darkness. His voice was warm and friendly, as if welcoming expected guests. Hassan and the two Kurds, who had now appeared again on the other side of the ditch, helped each person jump over to their side.

Kamal crossed last and shook hands with Hassan. 'I don't understand. This is a long way from Haj Ali's shop.'

Hassan nodded, smiling broadly. 'When I'm not fetching tea at Haj Ali's, I live here. The guides who brought you and those who will take you across to Turkey are from my village.'

A few hundred metres away, Kamal made out a cluster of mud houses similar to the ones he had passed earlier. The dogs had already started barking.

'I will take you to my house,' Hassan said, 'where you will eat and rest.'

Kamal had to bow his head slightly as he walked through the wooden gates that led to a small courtyard. A young woman in a colourful scarf with sequined edges was bent over a cooking pot on an open fire. The smell of steamed rice wafted from the pot. The woman straightened when she saw Hassan and the strangers.

'Bring some food for the visitors,' Hassan said. The woman bowed her head slightly, collected some dirty dishes in a bucket and took them over to a pump. She pumped water into the bucket and proceeded to scrub the dishes with a hard soap.

In the light of the fire, Kamal studied Hassan closely. He seemed different, taller perhaps. He did not walk with a bowed head as he did in Haj Ali's shop. He looked Kamal straight in the eye when he was talking to him. The guides and the woman treated him with deference and his house was larger than the others in his village.

'This way please,' Hassan took his shoes off and motioned for the others to follow him. The two guides had already gone through. Kamal peeled his mud-covered shoes off. There were a dozen pairs of shoes and slippers placed neatly in rows at the doorway. His head was groggy from lack of sleep and exhaustion. He could hear voices arguing inside but he couldn't make out what they were saying. Holding on to Behzad's hand he followed Hassan into the main room where several men sat cross-legged around a *sofreh*. They fell silent when they saw the strangers.

The room was lit by a naked light bulb suspended like a hanged man from the ceiling. The mud walls were white-washed and decorated with handwoven rugs. A collage of big and small rugs covered the floor.

'Please sit down,' Hassan offered. The men parted to make room around the *sofreh*.

'I'm tired, Baba,' Behzad yawned. Kamal looked down at his son who was leaning against his arm. His eyelids were so heavy with sleep he was struggling to keep them open. Kamal's chest tightened. Not for the first time, he began to doubt himself. He quickly pushed his thoughts away.

'Go to sleep if you like,' Kamal whispered into Behzad's ear. Behzad looked around the room at all the strangers wearing elaborate headdresses, with dark-lined, unshaved faces and dirt-stained nails. He shrank slightly and moved soundlessly into Kamal's lap, resting his head into his father's big armchair-like arms, and closed his eyes. His breathing fell quickly into a deep rhythm, the way children sleep when they trust their parents to keep them safe. Kamal, realising this, felt his chest tighten.

After supper, most of the men left and the women cleared away the *sofreh* before bringing out several thin mattresses and blankets. The whole time they kept their eyes diverted, careful not to make any eye contact with us. One of them smiled at Mum, sitting next to Behzad who was curled in a corner.

I leaned my head against the wall with my legs stretched out in front of me. I could hear Dad and Behrooz speaking, their voices drifting in and out of my consciousness.

'We'll put Nina and the kids in the middle,' Dad lowered his voice, as if worried he'd be overheard. 'You and I will sleep on either side in a V-formation. That way if anyone tries to get to the women, they'll have to climb over us first.'

I didn't understand what Dad meant by 'get to the women'. My exhaustion overcame me and I fell into a restless sleep.

It was still dark outside when Hassan and two other men switched on the light. Hassan's tone was business-like. His jaw was tense and his manner stiff. We sat up blinking into the light, trying to get our bearings.

'Get up. You have to go,' he said in a tight voice.

'Where to?' Dad asked, startled in the harsh light.

'Get up. We have to hurry. The Komiteh will be here soon.'

Outside, the cold air stung my face and made me shiver. I blinked several times to adjust my eyes to the darkness. Two men with blankets strapped to their backs motioned for us to follow them. We walked quickly past the mud houses and barking dogs. The sky had begun to change colour, making it easier to see ahead. Dad brought up the tail end with Behzad and one other guard. I heard him try to make conversation with the guard several times. Each time he was met with silence.

We walked over a hill. On the other side was a valley with large boulders clustered on either side. The men unpacked the blankets and gave them to us. 'Stay here,' one of the men said in a thick accent.

'How long are you leaving us here?' Dad grabbed the guide's arm as he turned to leave.

The man slowly but firmly removed Dad's hand. 'Hide behind these boulders. Stay quiet. It's dangerous for you.' He turned and the two guides quickly disappeared back over the hill.

It was windy in the valley. We had tried to shelter from the wind and stay hidden by crowding close together between a large group of boulders The wind pierced my skin through thin layers of clothes like needles piercing a pincushion. I buried myself under a blanket, leaning against a boulder, shivering.

Everything that had happened to us in the past twenty-four hours seemed surreal. It was all a dream. Soon I was going to wake up and find myself in Eshrat Mamman's room and I would tell her about my adventure. She would laugh and tell me I dreamt such nonsense.

But the sharp, cold texture of the rock, the wind and the sound of mosquitoes all told me this was not an adventure I could wake up from. We were going to live in another country where we did not know anybody. I would never see my home or sleep in my bed; I may never get to see my extended family again.

I shuddered and wrapped the blanket tighter around me.

The sun had moved higher in the sky, warming the valley and lifting everyone's mood. All morning the adults discussed what danger we might be in and what they would do if no one came back for us.

Eventually, we spotted two men in the distance walking in our direction. Dad tapped Behrooz on his shoulder and pointed to them. 'We'd better hide behind the boulders.'

From between the rocks we watched the men as they came closer. Each man carried a bundle at the end of a stick, which he balanced over his shoulder. They were heading straight towards the boulders.

Dad looked over to where Behzad and I had huddled next to Mum and pressed a finger against his lips. He moved further between the giant rocks and held his breath. The footsteps stopped on the other side of the boulders.

A man's head appeared from behind the first rock. '*Salaam, aleykom.*' Dad sighed in relief. He recognised the man as one of Hassan's guides.

'I've brought you some breakfast,' the man said. The men unwrapped their bundles. They had brought goat's cheese, stale bread and black tea that they poured out of a flask.

'How long must we stay here?' Dad asked between mouthfuls. 'Are the Komiteh coming?'

The man shrugged. 'Ask Hassan, Agha. He'll be here soon.'

After breakfast the men cleared away the food, making sure no crumbs were left behind. They left echoing the same chilling warning as before. 'You're in great danger. Make sure no one sees you.'

The sun was high in the sky, throwing short shadows when Hassan arrived.

'Hassan, what's going on?' Kamal asked as the two men shook hands. 'We've been waiting here all day and no one will tell us anything. My wife and kids are hungry and exhausted. Haj Ali told me we'd be walking for 500 metres. Last night alone, we must have travelled over ten kilometres. Look at the state of my shoes.' He pointed to his handmade shoes. 'They're falling apart from all the walking we've had to do.'

Hassan stifled a laugh. Kamal smiled too at his own naivety. He could see in Hassan's eyes that they were not the first people he'd seen wearing their best clothes to cross the mountains. They all believed Haj Ali when he told them how far they'd have to walk, and like Kamal they probably thought they might as well look respectable as they crossed the border. They too must have regretted their choice once their journey began.

'Agha Dastyari,' Hassan placed his right hand across his heart, 'be assured that we have you and your family's interest at heart. But . . .' he paused, 'we have a slight problem.'

Kamal's eyes dilated. 'What's the problem?'

Hassan motioned for Kamal and Behrooz to follow him up the hill. He dropped to the grass, lying flat on his stomach. He gestured for them to also get down, then he pulled out a pair of binoculars from his backpack, pressed them to his eyes and scanned the countryside. He pulled his binoculars away, squinted, pressed them to his eyes again and adjusted the knob until he found what he was looking for. Without taking his eyes away, he waved Kamal closer then moved aside, allowing Kamal to look through the binoculars.

'Can you see the truck?' he asked.

Kamal had trouble at first adjusting to the binoculars. He searched the area, pulling the binoculars away several times to get his bearings. He could see the dirt road, muddy in places.

He followed the road until he came to a part which dipped further into the sucking mud, and right in the middle of it he saw the truck. It stood lopsided with one of its back wheels embedded in the mud.

'That's the local Komiteh. They were on their way to our village last night when they took a wrong turn and got bogged in the mud. One of our watchmen saw them and ran back to warn us. That's why we had to get you out of my house and bring you here. It was for your own safety.'

Kamal's throat went dry. His fingers were trembling as he gave the binoculars to Behrooz.

'They've been stuck there all night,' continued Hassan. 'They have sent for men to help them pull the truck out.' Hassan fell silent. Kamal felt his hesitation.

'What else?'

'This road links us to the next village where another group is waiting to join us.'

'There was never any mention of us travelling with another group.'

Hassan raised his palm to pacify Kamal. 'They are a family, like yourselves,' he reasoned. 'They are stuck in the other village until this truck moves.' He paused and looked Kamal straight in the eye. 'We can't leave without them,' he said in a voice that did not encourage any arguing.

Kamal closed his eyes and pressed at his temples. Hassan noticed the strain around Kamal's eyes. 'Agha, Dastyari, over the past few months I have grown very fond of you. You always greeted me while most visitors ignored me, thanked me when I served you tea and never spoke down to me.' Hassan placed a hand on Kamal's shoulder. They were walking back towards the rest of the group.

'Do not worry,' he said in a lighter voice. 'The truck will be moved soon, we will get the other family here as fast as we can and, *inshallah*,' he said looking up to heaven, 'by tomorrow morning you'll be having your first breakfast in Turkey.'

Leaving on horseback

In the afternoon we watched a group of Hassan's men arrive and sit on the grass talking amongst themselves, waiting for the second party to join them. All except one were dressed in provincial headdress, cotton pantaloons and loose shirts.

The other man wore an ill-fitting Western-style suit that hung loosely on his skeletal figure. He sported a Fedora hat at an angle made fashionable by the 1940s Hollywood detective movies, and carried an umbrella, stabbing it in the dirt when he walked.

As the sun set, the activity on the hills increased. Men pulling donkeys loaded with heavy bundles went past and waved a greeting, not at all surprised by the odd mix of people gathered there.

'Who are these people?' Dad asked the man with the umbrella.

'Smugglers and merchants!' he said. 'These men have been trading along this route to Turkey for centuries. They do not recognise any borders created by governments in the big cities!'

The sky had turned peach and mauve when Dad spotted a group of people on horseback. 'Ah,' the man with the umbrella pointed to the riders. 'Looks like the Adliehs managed to get through.'

'Who are the Adliehs?' Dad asked, hoping to draw the man into conversation.

'Mr and Mrs Adlieh,' he said, nodding and smiling to himself. 'This is their second attempt.'

'What happened the first time?' Dad said with raised eyebrows.

'Agha Dastyari, the things I could tell you about these people! They have a lot of problems!' He swirled the air between them with his hand as he spoke. 'The first time we took them, Mr Adlieh's leg cramped after he got off the horse and we had to take them back.' A shadow of a smile stretched slowly across his face. 'Now they say they have practised and are fit to try again.'

'How old are they?' Dad was watching the horses with growing apprehension.

'Allah only knows. A man his age should die peacefully in his warm bed. It's that dragon he's married to.' The man wagged a finger, 'She'll be the death of him.'

I stood next to Dad, watching the arrival of the eight horses and their riders. The newcomers looked like a curious mix of escapees. Mr and Mrs Adlieh were as old as my grandparents. Mr Adlieh, a frail man in his eighties, sat erect on his horse looking nervously between the guides and us. His wife, a short robust woman with sagging breasts that hung low to the waist of her dress, eyed us with suspicion. A bald-headed, heavy-set middle-aged man, with thick glasses that kept slipping down his hooked nose, shifted uncomfortably in his saddle as he nodded and mumbled a greeting. Mr Adlieh introduced him as Khosro. The fourth was the Adlieh's youngest son, Reza. Reza was an energetic man in his late twenties with thick jet-black hair and a bushy moustache that covered his upper lip. He sat straight and confident on his saddle as he expertly rode the beast, showing off his skills to anyone who took notice.

I was excited and a little frightened by the sight of the horses. I had ridden on the beaches of the Caspian Sea, but those horses were old and broken. They walked with their heads down and at a donkey's pace. These horses looked strong and galloped fast like the ones in Westerns. I recognised some of the men with the Adliehs from the previous night.

Dad walked down and talked to some of them, offering them cigarettes. Behzad and I stayed close to Mum and admired the horses, throwing curious glances at our travelling companions.

'Agha Dastyari, this is my horse,' Hassan said, stroking the grey stallion's neck. 'It's the finest and strongest horse in the village.' He passed its rein over to Dad. 'I want you to ride it tonight.'

Dad's eyes widened. 'I can't ride. I've never been on a horse before,' he stammered. 'Not even those half-dead ones the kids ride on holidays.'

Hassan smiled and motioned for two of his men to help Dad. It took two attempts for him to get on the horse. Once on, he seemed surprised by how high he was. He pressed his eyes and said a silent prayer.

'God be with you,' Hassan said, extending his hand to shake Dad's.

Mum was helped onto her horse and, since they were a horse short, Behzad and I shared one. Behzad waved enthusiastically at Dad the same way he waved to the camera on horseback rides along the beach. Dad smiled back but I could tell he was worried.

The man with the umbrella called out and the horses, led by four guides, began to move. Dad's horse was at the head of the pack with Dad straining his neck every few minutes to look around for Mum and us. The sky had turned blue–grey and all was silent except for the soft, rhythmic tread of horses on the earth.

It wasn't bad at first, sharing a horse with Behzad. He was thin and fitted at the end of the saddle. I had pressed myself forward to give him more room. But after an hour of the horse shifting its weight from side to side, Behzad had started to complain about a lot of pressure on his groin.

'My doodool hurts,' he moaned in a small voice.

I pressed myself forward as far as I could go and searched amongst the shadowy figures ahead for my mum. The sky had turned the colour of dark steel with the only light coming from the moon struggling between the branches. I was too frightened to call out. Our guide had warned us not to make any noise.

Behzad moaned behind me. My heart ached for him. I bit my lip and decided to take a chance. 'Agha, how much longer?' I whispered to our guide.

He did not answer. I thought he might not have heard. I pulled on the harness, jerking the horse's head back. The horse shook his head and flared his nostrils. The guide turned towards me.

'Agha,' I said again, 'can you call our mother? My brother is in a lot of pain.'

He frowned and pressed a finger to his lips. Ahead, the group had slowed down. Every once in a while we stopped, and the man with the umbrella lit a cigarette and waved it. He waited, watching the mountain intently until he saw the signals he was looking for and we'd proceed forward.

I took the opportunity of the delay to try again. 'Please, Agha.'

He turned impatiently and took a few steps towards me.

'Agha,' I pleaded, 'can I take my brother to our mother?'

'Don't worry,' he said with a crooked smile, 'it won't be much further.'

He patted my leg and, to my horror, dragged his hand down my thigh to my knee and let it rest there. I felt his hand burn my skin through my clothes. I shook my knee slightly but his hand remained where he had rested it. I kicked the horse hard with my other leg and it jumped forward, startling the guide. He quickly moved away to calm it and I exhaled a broken breath.

Our group had started moving again. Behzad had gone limp behind me, his head resting on my back. His fingers were no longer locked around my waist.

'Behzad, are you okay?' I twisted one arm behind me, pressing him against me. His moans turned into a whimper.

I could hear frogs croaking and my heart sank. In the past hour we had crossed many ditches with streams running through them. The horses would step down into the ditch and then, with the help of the guides, leap out of them. Each time I heard the frogs, I held on to the saddle for dear life, convinced we were about to be thrown over the horse's head into the ditch. But this time I could hear something else.

The air on my arms stood erect when I realised it was the sound of rapids.

At this time of the year, the river was overflowing with melting snow travelling down the mountain. The man with the umbrella directed one of the guides to cross the river with Kamal's horse.

Kamal stared at the rapids with awe and great unease. The horse seemed nervous and reluctant to step in the river. Kamal could feel sprays of water descend on his skin like icy mist. He felt his pulse quicken as the man stepped gingerly into the river, holding the horse's reins in his hands. Halfway across, the icy water was up to his chest, making it difficult for him to balance against the force of the river. The man with the umbrella yelled at him, motioning him further upstream. The guide tried, pulling the horse behind him. Icy water lapped against Kamal's legs. He drew his legs up as far as he could. The sound of the raging water was deafening, its strength pressing them backwards. The horse was reluctant to move, neighing and stomping its front feet in the water. The guide pulled the horse with both hands and Kamal kicked it with his heels like he'd seen in movies to get it to move forward. Instead, the horse became further agitated and reared onto its hind legs.

Snap.

Kamal felt himself flying through the air in slow motion with the horse following. When he entered the cold river it was as if his body had been stabbed by a thousand knives. He resurfaced straightaway, disoriented, groping for something to hold on to. The rapids slashed against his face, blinding him. Between the roar of the river he could hear Nina yelling his name.

I heard Mum scream up ahead of us. Behzad lifted his head and looked in the direction of her scream. 'Kamal!' she screamed again. When we reached her, she was frantic. Her guide was trying to calm her.

'Sister, pull yourself together. They'll hear us,' he pleaded, trying to stop her from getting off her horse.

On the other side of the river, one of the guides was pulling Dad and his horse out of the river. The saddle sat lopsided on the horse's back.

'Kamal, take off your clothes before you die of pneumonia,' Mum screamed as she fought to free herself from the guide.

Dad stripped naked, covering his private parts with his hands. Meanwhile, the other guides had found a shallower path to cross upstream.

Mrs Adlieh started complaining to anyone who was willing to listen. 'Did you see that? We're all going to die tonight.' She beat at her head and body with her open palms.

'Calm down, woman,' her husband hushed. 'Nobody is going to die.'

'Didn't you see what happened?' she shrieked. 'How are we going to pass this river? Look at those rapids. He is fit and young.' She pointed across the river to where Dad stood naked. 'If we fall, it will be the death of us. We're all going to perish.' She continued beating herself. 'You,' she said pointing to the man with the umbrella, 'you'll have to answer to Allah if we die here tonight.'

He slowly turned and faced her, squaring his shoulders. 'You don't have to cross. You can stay here or turn and go back,' he hissed, narrowing his eyes. We were all close enough to hear every word and from the tone of his voice we knew he was willing to continue without them.

Our horse was the last to cross over. Our guide jumped on the back, sandwiching Behzad between us. He kicked at the horse and it galloped across the river. I held on to the saddle, frightened that I might slide off. It was both frightening and thrilling, feeling the rush of wind and the spray of icy water against my skin.

On the other side of the river, Mum was helping Dad into his light brown trouser pants and a dark jumper. He laughed nervously as he dragged his clothes over his nakedness.

The guides crowded around the broken saddle, each talking over the other. When Dad was dressed, he and Mum came over to see how we were doing.

'Behzad's not well,' I said and immediately my eyes filled with tears.

Behzad lifted his head slightly on hearing his name. 'Mummy!' he called out in a small voice, stretching his arms towards her. Dad helped Mum lift Behzad down.

'The saddle is too small for both of us. It hurts his penis,' I said, lowering my voice, embarrassed at mentioning my brother's private parts. I also wanted to tell them about that other thing with the guide, but felt too ashamed.

Mum pressed Behzad's face against her stomach, stroking his hair. She kept wiping at her eyes with her fingers. Dad went over to the guides and brought one back with him.

The guide shrugged his shoulders when Dad told him about Behzad. 'He has to cope.'

'He's about to pass out. Can't you do anything to help him?'

The guide shrugged again. 'He can sit behind the saddle,' he pointed to the rug thrown over the horse's back, under the saddle.

Behzad was reluctant to let go of Mum. 'I want to stay with you,' he pleaded.

'It won't be for long,' she said, biting hard on her lip. 'We're nearly over the border.'

'Promise?' he asked.

'Promise,' she said.

Behzad smiled and lifted his arms up so Dad could lift him back onto the horse.

The track narrowed into a steep hill covered in loose rocks. Below us we could see the road to the border. Once in a while we could see a car's dimmed headlights as it travelled along the dark road. The horses kept slipping on the small rocks.

'Hold tight to my waist,' I whispered to Behzad.

His round fingers tightened around me. The horse climbed, trying hard to steady itself. My fingers were going numb from holding on to the saddle so tightly. The horse surged forward, slipped, steadied itself and surged again. I held my breath every time it surged forward.

We were nearly over the top when the horse's back legs slipped from under it and it fell backwards on top of Behzad and me. The wind gushed out of me, leaving me breathless. Under me Behzad let out a stifled scream.

The horse quickly rolled onto its side and stood. Behzad and I lay where we had fallen, still a little dazed. One of the guides pulled us to our feet and told us to walk. I dusted Behzad off. Except for a few scratches he was fine. I took his hand and pulled him behind me.

The man with the umbrella walked over to Dad. 'Get off the horses.'

Dad climbed down unsteadily.

'Quickly!' the man with the umbrella ordered. 'You're a pathetic lot. Hurry up,' he snapped.

The guides had pulled down the luggage, food and water, and were dividing them between each person. They started arguing over one of Mrs Adlieh's bags.

'This one is too heavy,' one of the guides said in Turkish. 'It has to go back with the horses.'

Mrs Adlieh threw herself over the bag. 'This is all we have left in the world. Haj Ali promised us only 500 metres...'

'Quiet,' the man with the umbrella said. 'Stand aside, sister,' he commanded Mrs Adlieh. She did as she was told. He kicked the bag a couple of times. Something inside jingled. 'What are you carrying in here?'

'Nothing!' she said a little too quickly. 'Photos of my children and some clothes. Nothing of value to anyone else but me and my poor husband.'

Mr Adlieh dropped his eyes at the mention of his name. The man with the umbrella shook his head.

'No. We will not carry it.' Having made his decision, he turned on his heels and started to walk away.

'Noooooo,' Mrs Adlieh shrieked. She looked to the faces gathered around her. 'Please. Somebody help us.'

Kamal's throat tightened. He could not bear the thought of this woman's only remaining possessions being left on the mountain. He reached for his wallet. It was still wet from his fall in the river. He peeled 500 tomans from a bundle and offered it to the nearest guide. 'Take this and carry Mrs Adlieh's bag for her.'

The guide accepted the money, lifting the heavy bag over his shoulder.

'God bless you. You are a gentleman. You have saved us. May Allah's blessings forever shine upon you and your family.' She wiped her eyes with the corner of her scarf.

'That's not necessary,' Kamal said, a little embarrassed.

They began walking again. Kamal was bringing up the rear with Behrooz and Behzad. He felt more comfortable at the back, where he could keep an eye on his family. He had lost track of time. His watch was frozen forever on the time it had hit the freezing water. There seemed to be no end to the steep climb. His stomach grumbled and his throat was parched. In one hand he carried the family's bag and with the other he held on to Behzad's hand.

Behzad was slowing them down, with laboured steps. Once in a while he would stop to scratch his legs, never once letting go of Kamal's hand. They were falling behind the rest of the group. They turned a corner and found Khosro collapsed in the middle of the road like a wounded animal, and the man with the umbrella standing over him. The rest of the group stood in a semi-circle, frozen with fear.

'What's going on?' Kamal asked.

'This fat bastard won't move.' The man with the umbrella lifted his foot and kicked Khosro in the back. Khosro cried in pain, his hand shooting to cover where he had been kicked.

'I can't go on,' he gasped. 'Just go without me.'

'No one is going to leave you behind,' Kamal said, kneeling down next to him.

Khosro's breath wheezed, his large chest heaving with exhaustion. His face and bald head glistened with sweat.

'Leave me behind. Go without me,' Khosro said. He doubled over on his side as the man with the umbrella hit Khosro on the arms and legs with the wooden part of his umbrella. Khosro tried in vain to protect himself with his hands from the blows. He was like a giant sea lion, dragging his body awkwardly on land.

Kamal and Behrooz rushed to restrain the man with the umbrella. He freed himself from their grip, breathing hard, and stared angrily at Khosro whimpering in the dirt.

'If he stays here, he will be found in the morning,' he said to the frozen faces. 'They'll know we have passed through here and they'll come after us. It's your own funeral. You decide.'

A dozen pair of eyes waited for Kamal to make a decision for them. He sighed.

'Behrooz, will you take Behzad's hand?' Behrooz nodded and took custody of the small hand. Reza was helping his parents, which left only Kamal to help Khosro the rest of the way. He put his arm around Khosro's thick waist and helped him to his feet. He pulled Khosro's arm over his shoulder. Kamal's knees buckled as they adjusted to the extra weight.

Wordlessly, everyone filed behind the man with the umbrella and continued their slow march up the mountain.

Capture

I walked close to Mum, not wanting to be separated from her. The climb was becoming harder on her knees with steeper hills and bigger rocks to climb over. Below us, we noticed a group of floodlights. A few men with military uniforms milled around with their shotguns casually draped over their shoulders.

The man helping Mum over a large rock pointed to the lights. 'Iranian guards,' he said, pointing them out to us like a tour guide. 'We are now between borders.'

I looked down again at the men patrolling the border. One must have told a joke and they all laughed. We were so close they only had to look up with their lights to see us.

'Where is Turkey's border?' Mum asked.

He pointed to somewhere in the darkness. 'Just over those large rocks.'

Mum and I exchanged a knowing look. Mum unbuttoned her Islamic tunic and ripped off her headscarf. She threw them behind the rock she had just climbed over. She did it as an act of defiance, bunching her uniform and spitting on it. I followed her, feeling exhilarated. I moved to the front of the pack, crouching low like the guards.

In the thin light of the moon, we could just make out the three silhouettes bringing up the rear, the two taller frames on either side of the smaller one. Periodically, Behzad would stop, let go of Behrooz's hand and scratch his leg. He would then straighten, place his small hand back in Behrooz's and the three would resume their slow march. Khosro walked unsteadily on his own a few metres in front of them, labouring over every step.

In front of us was Turkey and an uncertain future; behind us Khomeini's Iran. Mum took one last look behind her, grabbed a patch of soil and dropped it in her pocket, then stepped into Turkey.

'*Dur! Dur!* Stop!'

The shout came from down the mountain and went through me like a cold knife. The whole world froze around us. The guide stood rigid for only a second, his senses on high alert. Then, like a flash, he started running up the mountain towards Iran. Uncertain and frightened, I followed him but my legs seemed to be moving in slow motion, and within seconds I had lost him. I was swallowed by darkness. I heard voices heading straight towards me. A cold sweat covered me. I started to run in the direction I thought I had come from. Back towards Iran.

A hand grabbed me and pulled me down behind a rock. *No!* A voice screamed inside my head. I struggled to get free.

'It's me. Mum,' she said.

I stopped struggling and collapsed in a fetal position on the cold earth with my head buried in my mother's soft belly. My body shook uncontrollably. Mum wrapped one arm around me, pressing me closer to her. After I calmed a little I realised we were not alone. Mrs Adlieh was sitting only a few inches away. I was surprised I had not seen her there. She was rocking her large body back and forth, pulling at the dirt with her nails and throwing it over her head and large breasts. Her eyes were pressed shut and her mouth was wide with grief.

'*Ayeeee!* We are going to die. *Ayeeee!*' she kept repeating like a chant.

'Shut up!' Mum hissed.

Mrs Adlieh did not pay any attention to her, continuing to beat her chest and rocking even harder. I buried my face again in Mum's lap. I heard the sound of heavy footsteps getting closer. A shout echoed around us. I bit down on my lip to stop myself from screaming. I was shaking again. I heard the soldier cock his rifle. He shouted again, paused and pressed the trigger.

The shot sliced through the air like a dagger. The large boulder we hid behind felt paper-thin as the vibrations shook it and the earth around us. I remained frozen, not daring to move.

A hand clasped the back of my shirt and pulled me upright.

'Mum!' I screamed, reaching back for her with outstretched arms. But another soldier was lifting her and Mrs Adlieh to their feet. Mum released herself from the soldier's grip and pulled me back towards her. The soldier let go of me without a struggle. They were surprised to find three women and stood staring at us.

Other soldiers had gathered the men in our group, but none of the guides were amongst them. A soldier went from one man to another frisking them. They hesitated when they got to us women. They had found nothing on the men and decided not to search us. Realising we had no weapons, the soldiers had relaxed but one of them still held a gun pointed at us.

Mrs Adlieh's cries had turned into a whimper. 'They will send us back. We are doomed,' she kept repeating to herself. 'We will be sentenced and executed.'

I wrapped my arms around my body to stop from shaking.

Mum's eyes searched the mountain. The soldiers talked briefly amongst themselves. They then motioned for us to start moving down the mountain. '*Yallah! Yallah!* Get moving,' they said, pointing with their muzzles to get us going.

'Mum...' I said, too frightened to finish the sentence. Neither of us had made an attempt to move.

'*Yallah!*' the soldier motioned for us to follow the others. We exchanged a look but neither of us wanted to move.

Dad and Behzad were missing.

Kamal, Behrooz and Behzad were hiding behind a large boulder. They were the last to cross the border into Turkey but had run back to hide behind the boulder when they had heard the soldier's shouts and saw the guides running past them. Behzad's head was limp against Kamal's chest. Kamal pressed his temple, his elbow resting on his knee. His head felt like exploding. He didn't know where his wife and daughter were.

A shot ran out, splitting through the tense silence. Bitter vile gathered in Kamal's throat. He turned to Behrooz.

'I have to cross the border,' he said almost apologetically. 'My wife and daughter are on the Turkish side. I have to find them.'

'I'll come too,' Behrooz said, shrugging his shoulders and smiling weakly. 'I have nowhere else to go.'

Kamal nodded, rose to his feet, lifted Behzad in his arms, and began to climb over the large rock and out of Iran for the second time.

'*Efendi*. Mate!' Kamal's voice echoed down the mountain.

Surprised, the soldiers quickly cocked their guns, pointing in the direction of the voice.

'*Efendi*,' Kamal called again in a shaking voice masked under a friendly smile. One of the soldiers flashed his light, searching the dark mountain for the source of the voice. Three lone figures, two men and a child, with their hands raised above their heads, walked towards the rest of the group. Behzad ran the last few steps unsteadily into Nina's arms.

Kamal could sense the soldiers were very tense. One soldier frisked them while another pointed a gun at their chests. He found Kamal's Swiss Army knife, rolled it a couple of times in his hand and, smiling, dropped it in his pocket. Kamal remembered the day he had bought it as a student in London. He had saved for weeks to buy it. He was courting Nina in those days, trying to stretch his meagre government allowance to take her out dancing. How innocent and carefree they were then. How far removed those days were from where they were now.

He tried to make conversation with the soldiers. Although they spoke Turkish, they spoke different dialects.

'Can I smoke?' he asked the man who was giving the orders.

The soldier nodded, relaxing a little. Kamal offered him a cigarette. The soldier shook his head. 'I don't smoke,' he said sheepishly.

Kamal patted his breast pocket for his matches. He must have lost them in the last part of the walk. The soldier got his own matches out and lit Kamal's cigarette. In the thin light of the flame Kamal was surprised to see how young the soldier was.

'You're a conscript?' Kamal asked. The soldier nodded.

'Where from?' The boy mentioned a town.

The name meant nothing to Kamal.

'It must be hard to be away from your family?'

'Yes, very.'

'I'll probably never get to see my mother again,' Kamal said staring at his hands. The soldier remained silent. After a pause he motioned for the group to start walking.

'Where are you taking us?' Kamal asked. There was a tight knot in his stomach.

'To the barracks.'

'What will happen to us?'

'You will be interrogated.' Sensing Kamal's fear, he added 'Do not worry. It's routine. We have to inform Ankara.'

'Will we be sent back?' Kamal asked, trying hard to stop his voice from shaking.

'You are a family. Your chances are better than if you were single men.'

The barracks

By the time we walked to the barracks the sky had changed colour again. The sun sat on top of the mountains like a giant fireball. We had been told to leave our bags on the mountain as they would be brought to us by the truck that carried the next sentry. Behzad walked the whole way with his eyes half-shut and his mouth slightly open. After twenty-four hours of running on adrenaline, his body had lost the will to stay awake and swayed from side to side. Dad and Behrooz held his small hands firmly in theirs. No one spoke as each person struggled with their own demons.

My head was filled with music. Not Mozart, Beethoven nor the Bee Gees. It was Maria and the von Trapp kids all clean and wholesome, dancing around Maria's bedroom, singing about raindrops and brown paper packages. On the mountains I'd pretended to be Liesl, running from the Nazis. But, hard as I tried, I couldn't imagine the von Trapp family looking like us: exhausted, dirty and defeated.

Inside the barracks, the Turkish soldiers woke up to find strangers amongst them. We followed one of the soldiers from the mountain down long narrow corridors. Light bulbs hanging from electric wires threw elongated shadows against the khaki-coloured walls. Soldiers passing us pressed themselves against the wall, staring curiously as we filed past them. I had never felt so ashamed, and kept my eyes downcast so as not to see them staring at us.

We were led into a brightly lit room that was partitioned in the middle by a glass wall. Two surprised soldiers jumped to their feet when we walked in. They spoke briefly to the one who had brought us, stealing glances at our group in-between conversation.

We waited while they pulled out forms, inkpads and small rectangular cards. Then we were led two at a time into the office, starting with the men.

'It's just like the movies, kids,' Dad chuckled, but his voice was tight.

It was soon my turn. The soldier took my right hand and, starting with my thumb, rolled it from side to side on the inkpad and then pressed it firmly on one of the ten boxes printed on the white card. He removed my thumb to reveal its print on the first box. He did the same for each of my fingers until all ten boxes had a clear imprint. We were being finger-printed like common criminals. I was choked with shame and humiliation.

In front of me, Mum kept glancing over her shoulder to where Behzad was getting his fingerprints done. His small frame was bent over, scratching the inside of his legs. Every time he stopped to scratch, his face was pinched in pain. The Turkish soldier waited patiently until he was ready to start again. Mum watched him with the studied eyes of a nurse and the worried expression of a mother.

Later, when we were waiting for our mug shots, Mum pulled down Behzad's pants, despite his protests. Her hand went to her mouth and she drew a quick breath. His inner thighs were covered in red, swollen fleabites.

Exhausted and hungry, we followed the soldiers to the mess hall. All conversations stopped as we filed past rows of tables full of soldiers towards two empty tables in the corner. We looked straight ahead, pretending not to notice the two dozen pairs of eyes focused on us.

Dad stretched Behzad over one of the tables and the rest of us crowded around the other. A soldier brought us a breakfast of bread, tea and goulash. Another brought Mum a thick pinkish ointment in a small bottle and some cottonwool which she smeared generously on Behzad's legs.

I ate my breakfast with little enthusiasm. My head throbbed with a dull ache and my eyes fought hard to stay open. Mrs Adlieh had started crying again.

'We're ruined. They will send us back for sure,' she sniffed and wiped her eyes with the corners of her scarf with ink-stained fingers. Her husband tried to console her.

'Didn't you hear what the soldier told Dastyari, they don't send back families.'

'We're ruined,' she took no comfort in her husband's words. 'I know it. I'll never get to see my children again.' She cried even harder, rocking her large frame over the bench.

After breakfast, Dad and Behrooz went to wash and shave. Dad had asked one of the soldiers for a shaving kit. Mum sat with one arm draped protectively over Behzad's sleeping frame. A kind soldier had brought blankets for us. I pulled one over my shoulders, folded my arms over the table and rested my head on top of it. I fell into a deep sleep full of dreams. In all of them we were escaping over the mountains.

Kamal splashed water over his face to wash off the last of the shaving cream. When he ran his fingers along his smooth skin, he smiled. He walked out of the bathroom a little taller and found Nina in the mess hall, stroking Behzad's sleeping face.

'What do you think?' Kamal asked.

Nina looked up, her eyes heavy with sleep. 'I can't believe how different you look,' she finally said, slightly slurring her words.

'You mean I don't look like an Islamic man anymore?' he said.

'No. I meant I think I got used to you with your moustache,' she said. 'It made you look...well...more masculine.'

Kamal touched where his moustache had been earlier. 'I wanted to wipe off all traces of the past few years,' he said in a tight voice. 'I just wanted to forget.'

Nina touched her husband's arm. Just then a soldier approached them and spoke to Kamal.

'The sergeant wants to talk to us,' Kamal told her.

The sergeant's office was a small, three by four metre room with a high ceiling, from which a lazy fan spun slowly. Behind his desk, the sergeant had hung a photo of Atatürk standing erect next to Reza Shah. Both men stared into the camera with hard eyes and unsmiling faces. On one wall, there was a large window overlooking a small cottage with a fenced-off garden. Three children played around a young woman who was hanging her washing on the line.

'My family,' the sergeant said with a smile when he saw Nina looking at them. He then shook Kamal's hand with a firm grip.

The sergeant was a slim man in his late thirties with thin black hair receding around his temples. He motioned for Nina and Kamal to take a seat. Shortly after, Behrooz, the Adlieh family and Khosro walked in, dragging their heavy suitcases behind them.

'I know about the rumours that we send people back,' the sergeant began in a paced and measured way. 'We are aware of the dangers to those released to the Iranian authorities and we are sympathetic to them.' He leaned over his desk, spreading his fingers as a mark of his sincerity. 'However, we do have to send your documents along with your fingerprints and a report to Ankara. If they agree, you will be given permission to be escorted to Istanbul where you can catch a plane out. You will not be allowed under any circumstances to leave Istanbul to travel to other parts of Turkey.'

He paused, allowing Kamal to translate to the others.

'What happens if they don't give us permission?' Kamal asked.

The sergeant shifted forward in his seat as if not comfortable with what he was about to say. 'If Ankara refuses your entry, or if you are caught leaving Istanbul without authorised permission, you will be handed back to the Iranian government.'

Kamal's voice shook as he translated to the group. There was a pause, as each person slowly digested the possibility of his or her worst fears coming true.

'As for your valuables,' the sergeant broke the silence, 'it will be best if you hand them all over to us.'

Kamal shifted in his seat. Mrs Adlieh exchanged nervous glances with her husband.

'I will document everything,' the sergeant said, sensing the group's unease. 'And I will give you a receipt for all your valuables.'

Kamal and Nina locked eyes. She shrugged her shoulders and nodded in agreement. Kamal walked to where the bags had been piled in a corner. He ripped the lining with little effort and pulled out the rolls of American dollars and British pounds. The sergeant counted the money and gave him a receipt for them. The money was placed in an envelope, marked and sealed just like Kamal had seen on cop shows when a prisoner is being admitted.

Next to him, Mrs Adlieh was opening the locks on her bags with a key she wore around her neck. On top of the bags there were clothes and some toiletries. She lifted them to reveal, to the astonishment of Nina and Kamal, a rolled-up silk carpet. She removed the carpet with some difficulty. From between its folds a pile of silverware tumbled out. She slowly stood up, avoiding Kamal's glare.

The sergeant was not surprised as he documented the items, reading them out one by one, waiting for Kamal to translate and then asking for a signature. Then he picked up a series of forms already laid out in neat folders on his desks, and checked their headings before selecting one form per family.

For the next two hours Kamal answered questions and translated for the others.

Who are you?

Where do you live?

What is your profession?

Do you have any children?

What are their names?

How old are they?

Are you a communist?

What are you doing in Turkey?

Who brought you here?

What were their names?

Kamal hesitated briefly before giving out Haales's and Esmat's names.

Where did you meet them?

Do you or anyone in your family have ties with the Islamic fundamentalists?

What is your religion?

Where are you heading?

Do you have a visa?

Why did you escape from Iran?

Do you have a criminal record?

Do you take drugs?

Are you carrying any drugs?

Between questions strong hot bitter tea was served, and every so often Nina quietly slipped out to check on the kids, still asleep on the hard benches. Their faces were relaxed and their breathing rose and fell rhythmically. Watching them huddled together made Nina's chest tighten in a knot. She blinked back the tears gathering behind her eyes and retraced her steps to the sergeant's office.

Dubayazid

That evening we were gathered in the sergeant's small office.
Behzad was asleep with his head leaning against Mum's chest.
Through the tiny window the sky had turned from blue to a palate
of orange and blood pink. A wafer thin moon moved higher in
the sky as the sun made its slow descent behind the mountains.

Two officers stood behind the sergeant. One of them, the
older and more higher ranked of the two, looked unsteady on
his feet and kept having to support his weight against the back
of the sergeant's seat. His freshly shaved face was flushed and
his eyes looked slightly glazed as if he were about to nod off.
His deputy stood close to him, throwing nervous glances in
the direction of his senior officer.

The sergeant introduced him as the commander of the
police station in Dubayazid, a small town nearby where we were
to be transported. We were to stay there while officials in the
capital, Ankara, examined our documents.

While the sergeant spoke the commander's eyes moved from one person to the next. He allowed his eyes to rest on me a little longer. My cheeks burnt hot and I pressed closer to my mum. From the corner of my eyes I noticed his lips turn slightly upwards as if pleased by my embarrassment.

The sergeant handed our possessions over to the police commander and all parties signed documents confirming the exchange. As we were leaving, the sergeant handed Dad his Swiss Army knife and Behrooz his sunglasses.

'I believe my men took these from you on the mountain.'

'Thank you,' Dad said, 'I will not forget your kindness.'

'Allah be with you,' the sergeant said, shaking Dad's hand firmly.

Outside, Kamal lit a cigarette. The commander's whisky breath, his unsteady step as he walked to the waiting jeeps, and the pentrating glare directed at his daughter had left Kamal feeling uneasy. He didn't want to sit in the same jeep as the commander but the Adliehs were already climbing into the second vehicle. There would not be enough room for them all and he wanted to keep his family together in one jeep where he felt he could protect them better.

Nina climbed into the backseat with the kids, while Kamal and Behrooz took the middle seats. They rode in silence with the deputy driving along the bumpy road. The headlights sliced through the darkness as the noise of the engine filled the otherwise peaceful countryside.

The police commander turned in his seat to face his passengers. He offered the men a cigarette. Kamal accepted, keen to establish rapport.

'What's your relation to one another?' he asked in a raspy voice.

Kamal told him. The commander wanted to know each person's name.

'Banafsheh. That's a pretty name.' He pulled a torch from the glove box and aimed the glaring light at the backseat. 'How old is she?'

'She's just a child,' Kamal said after a long pause, 'she's not even thirteen yet.'

Nina shifted in her seat. She could clearly sense Kamal's tension and was worried by the attention her daughter was receiving.

'I don't believe she's your daughter,' the commander said in a stony voice. 'She looks much older than twelve.'

Kamal swallowed hard. 'I . . . I can assure you,' he stammered.

'Sir, they are a family,' the deputy interrupted, lowering the commander's arm holding the torch. 'Remember your duty to Allah and as a Muslim. It is a sin to interfere with another man's family.'

'She's not his daughter,' the commander retorted. 'He's lying.'

He became more and more agitated, picking up his torch and aiming it at the backseat again.

He started to yell in Turkish, *'Atta-sin? Atta-sin?'* He yelled it over and over while pointing to Kamal. Kamal was frightened and confused, trying hard to reason with the commander.

Eventually, it seemed to work because the commander switched off his torch and turned to face the front while mumbling under his breath. He lit another cigarette and drew angrily, burning it down to its filter. He wound down the window and threw the cigarette out, the red glow disappearing in the pitch black night. The deputy was speaking to him, calming him down.

My head felt like shattered glass and I was nauseous. I closed my eyes and breathed deeply, hoping to push the nausea back down. Behind my closed eyelids red, jagged lights flashed like speeding traffic. I wished for sleep, for my bed with the purple blanket my grandmother had knitted for me. I wanted to wake up and discover everything that had happened in the last forty-eight hours was nothing more than a dream, an adventure from the depths of my imagination.

I pressed my forehead against the window, feeling the vibrations of the jeep. I became aware of the sounds around me. The humming of the engine, the bounce of the suspension over potholes, the changing of gears, my parents' whisperings, the shifting of the commander in his seat, the squealing of the window as it reluctantly rolled down further, the gushing of wind, a click, the deputy shouting, 'Commander!' and gunshots.

The jeep braked hard, swerved and stalled at the side of the road. My body rolled into a fetal ball with my palms pressed hard to my ears.

Bang. Bang. Bang.

The commander continued to empty his ammunition out into the night sky. Beside me, Mum let out a scream before reaching for the startled Behzad and pressing his small frame into hers.

The deputy pulled at the commander's arm, shouting at him to stop. The second jeep had stopped behind us, flooding our vehicle with its headlights. With one last effort the deputy pulled the commander's arm away from the window. He didn't resist, having run out of ammunition. He turned and flashed Dad an angry look before replacing his gun in his belt.

One of the soldiers in the second jeep walked up to the deputy's window. The deputy spoke to him, keeping his tone light, but his laughter was forced and the soldier hesitated until the commander yelled and motioned for him to go back.

In the thin light I saw the deputy blink several times before he turned the ignition. The car groaned into life. He put the car into first gear, released the brake and we were back on the bumpy road.

We drove through a small village in total darkness, past shadowy buildings with dim lights in their windows. I was jealous of the people there, for having their own homes, their own friends, and their normal lives. I felt as if I was driving into an abyss. I wanted to go back. At home we were somebody; our family and friends loved us. We knew and belonged somewhere. Here we were nobodies, unwelcome foreigners, whom at best must be tolerated and pitied. The shame of it burned me. I did not want to be pitied or be at the mercy of people I didn't know or trust.

I looked over at Dad's tired and ashen face. Why did we leave our lives behind? I knew there were desires in him I did not yet understand: his passion in the initial days of the revolution, and later the strain around his eyes when he looked through his *TIME* magazines all blackened and ripped by the censors' marker. I had seen the anger that flashed in his eyes when I told him about the subjects that I had to do in the new school curriculum: Islamic theology instead of history, Koran recitals, and political law of the Islamic Republic.

My parents carried their guilt, their shame and their fears like heavy burdens on their backs. A burden so heavy that it stooped their shoulders, crushed their spirits and gagged their dreams. Maybe they saw no other alternative but to leave.

Polici Agri

We arrived at a small police station. The sign said 'POLICI AGRI'. Agri was a small suburb outside of Dubayazid. We carried our bags across the tiled foyer to a large common room with fold-out tables and black vinyl cushioned chairs. Two officers were playing ping-pong in the corner. They stopped when they saw us.

At the end of the hall there was a wooden bookcase. With the exception of a few books, the shelves were empty. In the middle of it, a small black and white television was showing football with a group of officers around it. They cheered loudly as a player scored but quickly fell silent when they saw us.

The deputy spoke to one of the officers who nodded and, along with another officer, helped us with some of the heavier bags. We followed them down a wide spiral staircase. The black and white peppered tiles reminded me of the ones in my grandmother's house. My eyes clouded over with the image of her crouched down on the same tiles, crying and beating her chest, on our last night together. I blinked, forcing the tears back.

I took the stairs slowly, one at a time behind Dad, who carried Behzad in his arms, down to the area we later nicknamed the 'Dungeon'.

It was dark except for a dim light from a single fluorescent tube that occasionally flickered and buzzed. The deputy led the group to one end of the corridor.

Kamal stood in front of an iron door with a small barred window while one of the officers fumbled with a set of keys. Fear flashed through him. Will they lock us up in here? The officer chose one of the two long metal keys on the ring, tested it and smiled when he heard the clink. The door groaned open. The deputy switched on the light. Behind Kamal, Mrs Adlieh let out a stifled scream.

In a four by three metre cell with grey damp walls and no windows, stood three large double bunks. On top of each a thin mattress was rolled up next to a set of sheets and a blanket. Nina's hand went to her face, covering her mouth and nose. The place smelled of unwashed bodies, mould, stale urine and fear. With no windows or door to escape from, the smells had settled on the mouldy grey walls and mattresses.

Kamal stared around the small cell in disbelief. A knot grew and twisted inside him.

'Allah be willing, you will not be staying here for long,' the deputy said. He fumbled with his keys as he spoke, not able to look Kamal in the eye.

Kamal nodded, unable to speak.

'Where are the bathrooms?' Nina asked.

'This way,' said the deputy, stepping out of the doorway.

In the corridor an officer was escorting another prisoner towards the cells. The prisoner had his right arm in a sling. His hair was dishevelled and his clothes were crumpled. He walked with sunken eyes fixed on the floor. As he got closer he lifted his eyes to look at the new inmates. Dark hollow rings around his large brown eyes made them protrude even more. The officer unlocked the cell opposite and locked it again behind the prisoner.

'Who's in that cell?' Kamal asked.

'Mostly nomads and shepherds with little understanding of borders,' the deputy said with a shrug of his shoulders. 'That one...' pointing to the prisoner who had just passed them, 'he's a communist!' The deputy spat out the words as if removing something vile from his mouth.

He walked Kamal and Nina to the other end of the corridor where the prisoner had just been escorted from. The smell of urine was overpowering. Nina's hand automatically went to her face again. There were two porcelain sinks with only a tap for cold water. A small cracked mirror hung above each one. Kamal watched as Nina checked her fragmented reflection in the mirror. Her skin had a greenish tone under the naked bulb. She turned the tap to splash some water over her face. The pipes groaned and rattled in protest and finally vomited out bursts of icy water into the sink.

Behind them were three squat toilets in wooden cubicles with doors that didn't close properly, each with a small watering can for washing. The urinals stood in a row behind the cubicles. There was no toilet paper, no showers and no privacy.

Nina looked at Kamal with liquid eyes.

'I'm sorry, honey,' he said. 'I'll make it up to you.'

'I'll be fine,' she said, forcing a smile.

Kamal stood guard, watching while Nina, with stooped shoulders, threaded her steps through the puddles on the floor. She looked in each cubicle and eventually chose one. With a last look at Kamal, she went in and gently closed the door behind her.

Kamal lit a cigarette and felt a pain like hot coals on his heart.

We spent a restless night cramped in our cell. The door was locked but we were told we'd be free to come up to the common room in the morning. The men had pushed the beds together, and we slept huddled next to one another. I could hear Mum crying next to me. She had Behzad cradled in her arms with her back to me, but I could feel her shoulders shaking and hear her sniffing. So did everyone else. There was no room for privacy in the Dungeon.

Just before drifting off to sleep I heard my parents whispered voices talking about the commander and the conversation that had passed between them in the jeep. I heard Dad tell Mum that as long as we stayed together, we should be safe, but all the same, she should not let me wander off on my own to the toilets or anywhere else. Their conversation moved on to how they could contact their family back in Iran before I fell into a deep sleep, dreaming of playing in my bedroom with my cousin.

'The commander wishes to speak to you,' the deputy told Kamal when he unlocked the door in the morning.

Kamal's temples throbbed as he climbed the steps behind the deputy. In his office the commander sat with red puffy eyes behind a modest desk. He stood when Kamal entered the room.

'I wish to apologise for my behaviour last night,' he said, looking Kamal in the eye as he shook his hand. 'It was not appropriate behaviour.'

'I appreciate your apology,' Kamal said, trying to hide the surprise from his voice.

'I hope your stay here will be comfortable. Hassan, the young boy who does errands for us, will buy your food every day. He can be a little temperamental. Tell my officers if he gives you any trouble. You may use the common room during daytime, but at night you will sleep in your cell downstairs.' He paused briefly before asking, 'Do you have any questions?'

Kamal shook his head.

'*Inshallah*, your papers will arrive shortly from Ankara,' the commander shook Kamal's hand again, giving him a slap on the back.

After that meeting, Kamal was asked to act as translator for the others and to help them fill out form after form. He complained about their situation often. Every day he scaled the steps to the commander's office. He figured the more he complained, the more eager they would be to have their transfer approved quicker. To his credit the commander listened, mostly out of guilt from the first night, and complied with Kamal's requests.

One time Kamal made an official complaint to the Red Crescent, the Islamic Red Cross, that, as a Muslim man, he was required to wash himself once a week and there were no facilities for them to do so in the police station.

The commander arranged for several non-uniformed police to escort the group in twos and threes to the *hamam* at the barracks. The men were ushered into a small century-old bathhouse with grey stone walls and small windows large enough to allow in natural light and high enough to keep in the heat. They stood naked, waiting for the water to be boiled and poured down through the labyrinth of pipes and out small holes in the wall where they caught the water in wooden bowls, pouring it over their heads and shoulders. The steaming liquid was delicious against their dirty skin. Kamal soaped himself and Behzad quickly. Behzad complained about Kamal's rough hands washing his hair, but even he seemed to enjoy himself. Fifteen minutes later the water had trickled and stopped and Kamal asked for towels.

'No towels,' the guard said. Kamal picked up his belongings, took Behzad's hand firmly in his and, with his head held high, walked out to the great cheer of a dozen soldiers waiting to use the *hamam*. Two towels appeared and they were quickly wrapped in them. Cleaned and dried they waited in the sun to be transported back to the police station. For those few minutes, with the sun warm on his back and the smell of shampoo in his hair, Kamal almost felt like a normal person again.

—◊—

The girl was the same age as me. Her wet hair fell in clumps around her face as she bent forward and sniffed the yellow tub containing my facial scrub. She smiled and sniffed again, pleased with the citrus smell. It was my first experience at a public bath, even though Dad had often entertained us with stories of childhood visits to the baths with his mother and siblings.

When we first arrived I had clung to Mum, frightened by the tall stone walls and the curious looks of the local women. I was reluctant to undress in front of them. Slowly the friendliness of the women and the hot water on my skin eased my tension. The older women with sagging breasts crowded around Mum and tried to help her wash her clothes. The women chatted to her with a combination of words and hands as they scrubbed, rinsed, wrung and hung the clothes on a rope to dry. They opened her jars of facial creams and tried it on their rough skins, asking Mum questions she could not understand.

The girl next to me wanted to try my scrub. I scooped a small amount on my fingers and scrubbed her face in small, circular motions the way Mum had taught me. She giggled as my fingers travelled across her face. By the time I had poured the warm water over her cheek, a group of girls had gathered around us. She touched her cheek with the back of her hand and smiled broadly. One of the other girls had picked up the tub and wanted to try it. I nodded that she could and soon they were all sticking their fingers into it.

By the time we left the bathhouse there was nothing left of my scrub. The women kissed and hugged us, wishing us well in a language we did not speak.

—ɷ—

Kamal walked the long corridor to the commander's office. This time his complaint was on behalf of the men in the opposite cell who had not eaten for several days. He chose to make his complaint at the time when he knew the commander received his dinner from home. With soft eyes, the commander had pushed his plate away and asked his deputy to send his dinner to the three prisoners to share.

Tuvalet

I was in deep concentration over my next move. Across the table sat one of the policemen. He had a stupid smile on his face. Every time he smiled, which was often, his lips parted so wide his smile seemed to cover his whole face. He had a reason to smile. He was beating me convincingly in backgammon. Backgammon had never been my forte but, even so, I hated losing. He pointed to the board, still smiling, motioning for me to make my next move.

I had not noticed it at first, the thick liquid movement between my legs. I was not expecting it. When I did feel it, I first thought it was sweat from sitting too long on the vinyl chair. As I strained to make my next move, the chatter inside my head intensified. When I finally realised what it was, I froze in my seat. Blood rushed to my head, burning my cheeks. My eyes darted around the common room for Mum. As if by instinct her eyes lifted to mine at the same time. The expression she saw on my face made her stand up and cross the room in quick steps. I heard my opponent say something. From the tone of his voice I figured he was asking me if I was all right. I heard the word 'okay' as a question. I ignored him as I pulled Mum's arm down and whispered in her ear.

My voice was filled with tears ready to be spilled at any moment. A deep shame seared through me turning my cheeks a deeper shade of red.

Mum's eyes softened. 'That's nothing to worry about. From the look in your eyes I thought it was something serious.' She stroked my hair and face. She took my hand. Her hands were soft and cool. 'Come with me downstairs and I'll fix you up.'

I sat glued to the chair, afraid to stand up. Mum sensed my hesitation. 'I'll walk close behind you. No one will notice.'

That was not all I was worried about. I knew what Mum had packed in her toiletry bag and there were no pads in there. As we stood to leave, the policeman also stood. His eyes searched our faces, wondering if somehow this was his fault. I avoided his gaze but Mum smiled, reassuring him that I was okay.

Thankfully, the bleeding had not been much and my period was over after a couple of days just as unexpectedly as it had started. Mum taught me to make crude homemade pads with cottonwool and tissues. They were lumpy and uncomfortable, and I hated wearing them.

The same policeman sought Mum and I out a few days later. We were watching television. *Dallas* was on and we were already hooked after two episodes. Morgan Fairchild, with puffed-out, overbleached hair, pointy nose and pursed lips, glared at her lover who had betrayed her. It was dubbed in Turkish. Sometimes

Dad translated but mostly we followed the action and guessed the dialogue. It gave us something to talk about afterwards.

The young policeman stood to the right of the television screen wearing a wide smile. He rocked up and down on the balls of his feet like a kid with a secret he couldn't hold any longer. We turned to look at him, a little annoyed by his timing. From behind him he pulled out the metal skeleton of a chair. The vinyl back was still on it but the seat had been screwed out. He presented it to us like a gift and then took a step back so we could marvel at it. Mum and I stared at it, wondering what we were meant to do. We smiled politely, eager to get back to our soap opera. Noticing our confusion he tried to demonstrate by sitting theatrically on it. By now, others had gathered around us like participants in a game of charades.

'*Tuvalet!*' he said and we finally understood.

Despite squat toilets being common in Iran, our family had been used to the European-style of toilets. Dad must have mentioned it to him in passing and he had invented this homemade version for us.

'*Gall, gall,*' he motioned for us to follow him. His wide smile grew even larger as he picked up his invention and headed for the stairs to the Dungeon. We reluctantly abandoned *Dallas* and walked after him, followed by Dad, Behzad, Behrooz, the Adliehs and other off-duty policemen. In the toilets, he walked into the first cubicle. He placed the four metal legs of the seat over the squat toilet, shook it to make sure it was secure, and then stepped out, holding the door open.

'*Buyuruz,*' he invited us to try it.

I shifted my weight and felt a rush of blood to my cheeks. A few awkward moments passed before Dad suggested they should all go back upstairs to give us a little privacy. Mum and I were then left alone in the middle of the toilets.

'You go first, honey,' Mum stifled a laugh, 'I'll try it a little later.'

The metal bars were cold. I was past caring whether they were clean or not. It was a relief not to have to balance myself on unsteady legs. I had not had any motion in my bowels since we had left Iran over a week ago. I sat and waited. I thought of songs. 'Here Comes the Sun' by the Beatles was one. Then 'Favourite Things' from *The Sound of Music*, but I stopped that quickly because it reminded me too much of the night on the mountains.

My motion came in one big hard lump, leaving my body with great reluctance. I felt like I was being ripped apart as it inched its way out slowly. After long minutes of pushing, it fell on the porcelain with a great thud. My bottom felt tender and grateful for the cold water I used to wash with. I felt lighter as I stood to pull the long metal flush. It rolled hesitantly towards the sewer hole and to my horror got stuck at the mouth of it. I flushed the toilet several more times, but it just made a gagging sound, refusing to clear the content.

I pulled my pants up and, after checking that no one was around, rushed to the basin to fill the watering can which I poured into the toilet. It did nothing. I threw more water on it, pulled the metal chain again and again.

Nothing.

I tried to think of another way. All the alternatives I thought of were too repulsive but I could not just leave it there. I picked up the watering can, holding it in my hand like a weapon. I first prodded then pushed at it until it finally gave way and disappeared down the black hole. My face was screwed up in revolt and I had to take a few deep breaths to hold back the vomit that threatened to projectile.

I washed the watering can with soap and scrubbed my hands three times until they were pink from all the rubbing. Thankfully no one noticed me as I slipped into the hall and took my seat next to Mum.

Behzad bent low over the ping-pong table, fighting his disappointment at losing the game.

'Match point,' I said and served the ball. It bounced low over the net, touched the edge of the table and bounced to the floor. I chased after it crashing into tables and chairs.

'I win,' I said, not hiding my pleasure at beating him.

'No, you didn't. That ball was out,' he said. 'I don't want to play with you anymore, you're a cheat.' He threw the wooden bat on the table and sulked to the corner of the room where Dad and Khosro were playing backgammon.

I stared after him, now I had no one to play with. Behzad sank into a seat next to Dad, resting his head on Dad's shoulder. He looked back over his shoulder at me, his eyebrows knitted into a tight twist. 'I'm never going to play with you again.'

There weren't many people in the mess hall that afternoon. I motioned to one of the young guards, asking whether he wanted to play. He nodded and I passed him the ball to serve.

None of us noticed the officer who walked into the hall. We had never seen him before. He was tall, with a bushy moustache that covered his entire upper lip and eyes bright with anger. He covered the distance between the door and the ping-pong table in three long strides and started shouting at the guard. The guard dropped the bat on the table, gave a stiff salute to the officer before running out into the corridor.

The air in the room was stretched tight with tension. I slowly backed away from the table and moved closer to where Dad was slowly rising from his seat. All eyes were on the officer and he stared back at us with open hatred. My heart was doing somersaults inside my chest. Behzad squeezed himself in the small space between Dad and the wall. His small hand looked lost inside Dad's large fist. He flashed me a look filled with fear and confusion.

'*Efendi*,' Dad began holding out his free palm in the air between them.

Footsteps were running down the corridor towards us. The deputy ran breathless into the room, followed closely by the guard. The officer turned and began shouting at them. The deputy tried to calm him, but the more he tried the more agitated the officer became. The deputy had placed himself between us and the officer. The officer's face had turned crimson. He pushed the deputy out of his way, pulled out his pistol and aimed it at us. Blood iced in my veins and I started to shake. Tears stung the corners of my eyes and I looked over to Dad for help.

'*Efendi*,' Dad said in a shaky voice. 'We are a family. We are not criminals. Please put the gun away, you are scaring the children.'

'He is right,' the deputy said, reaching slowly to lower the officer's arm. 'They are a family, educated in England. They are not like those communists. Put down your gun.'

The officer shrugged off the deputy. 'What do you think this is? A holiday camp for the Iranian refugees? They have no right to be here. Take them downstairs and lock them up in their cell. They are forbidden to come up here again.'

Downstairs Mum was washing a few clothes in the bathroom sink. Her fingers had turned pink from scrubbing under the icy water. Behzad and I ran to her, burying our faces in her chest.

'What's the matter?' she asked dropping the shirt she was washing in the sink. 'Why are you crying?' She combed Behzad's hair with long strokes.

'*Yallah!*'

Blood drained from Mum's face as she looked up and saw the gun. Her mouth opened in a silent scream but the sound remained frozen in her throat.

'*Yallah!*' the officer said again, motioning with his gun that he wanted us out of the bathroom.

Mum picked up the washing and walked past the officer in a wide arc. Behzad and I each held on to one of her arms. At the end of the corridor, Dad and the others were being led to our cell as well.

The cell door clanked loudly behind us followed by the cold echo of the key turning in the lock. Frightened Behzad and I burst into fresh tears. Mum held us in her arms murmuring assurances.

Dad paced the cell like a caged animal. He turned and banged hard on the metal door with both palms.

'We are not animals,' he yelled through the bars of the small window. 'We are families. You cannot treat us like this.'

He continued to yell, his voice bouncing off the empty corridor. At first, no one tried to stop him. Each person sat in a corner of the bunks, either staring at a dark patch on the floor or shedding silent tears. After a while Behrooz tried to pull him away, but Dad shook him off and continued to bang against the cell door, shouting to let us out. Finally exhausted, his voice drained, he sank to the floor, dropping his head in his hands.

We did not eat that night. Dad translated what had passed between the officer and the deputy in the mess hall. The next day one of the police guards opened our cell. Still shaken from the experiences of the previous day, we were not sure if we were allowed to leave the cell or whether we were being transported to somewhere else. We looked to Dad for directions but he sat motionless on his bed. The guard cleared his throat self-consciously and left us, leaving the cell door open. After what felt like a long time Dad straightened himself up and walked through the narrow door, the rest of us filing wordlessly behind him.

We never saw the officer from the previous day again. We found out from some of the friendlier guards that he was from a nearby village and was here due to a complaint by one of the guards about the 'freedom' we were enjoying at the station. The officer had threatened to lodge a complaint to Ankara about the station's lax dealings with the illegal refugees. He claimed our 'freedom' would encourage the refugees to pour over the border where they could have a good time at the expense of the Turkish people.

Kamal had gone to the cell to get his cigarettes. He walked in on the Adliehs and Khosro talking in a huddle. They stopped when he entered. An awkward pause hung heavy in the air as Kamal got his cigarettes and walked out again. But he didn't go back upstairs. Instead he stood outside the cell with his back pressed against the wall, careful not to be seen.

'I might be able to help you get a passport for your son,' Khosro said inside. Kamal heard the bed creak as Khosro got up and took a few heavy steps. 'There's an Iranian man in Istanbul,' he was unzipping a bag and rummaging through it.

Kamal patted his pants and found a pen.

'This man has a reputation for carrying a few policemen in his hip pocket,' Khosro continued as he looked through his bag. 'I've got his name somewhere here... There it is.' Kamal scratched the name and phone number on the inside of his cigarette packet, closed it and silently ran up the stairs, taking two at a time.

Istanbul

While we were stuck at the police station, other than the uncertainty, the worst part was the boredom. Our days were spent playing cards, ping-pong or backgammon, and reading the Koran for the officers. From three o'clock in the afternoons, the black-and-white television came to life. For a few hours before we were locked up for the night, Hollywood and Turkish soap operas filled the void of our daily humdrum.

After fourteen nights punctuated by feelings of helplessness, uncertainty, boredom and a deep yearning for personal space, the commander asked Kamal to his office.

'I have received word from Ankara today that you and your family have permission to cross the country to Istanbul.'

A small burning fire stirred inside Kamal, slowly spreading its warmth all over his body. 'When can we leave?' he asked.

'As soon as you like,' the commander said. 'However, two civilian-clothed officers will be escorting you and you'll need to pay for their fares as well as your own.'

'What will happen to us in Istanbul?'

'Your documents will be passed to the authorities over there. I must warn you again not to leave Istanbul and travel to other parts of Turkey under any circumstance.'

Kamal knew he had to go to the Australian Embassy in Ankara to have their visa stamped in their passports. 'What happens if we do?'

The commander's features darkened. 'You will be arrested and then handed over to the Iranian government. What will happen to you then...' His words trailed off, leaving a big question mark in the air.

The small aircraft started to taxi, gathered speed and took off. It was late afternoon and we had been travelling on a bus for most of the day through endless poppy fields. Behrooz and two officers, one of whom snored loudly behind me, were travelling with us. The hostesses in their smart navy uniforms served light snacks. It was still a little strange for me to see women in public places with make-up and no hejab. One of them offered me a tray. I shook my head. For some reason I felt embarrassed to look at her. She looked too beautiful, too uncovered.

Next to me, Behzad was asleep, his chest rising and falling in a peaceful, rhythmic pattern. The rash on his legs had almost healed. In the past two weeks he had adapted well to his new surroundings, making friends with the police officers and enjoying the undivided attention of both Mum and Dad. It was his loss of weight and stretched skin that hinted the experience had not been easy for him. I closed my eyes, hoping I'd also fall into a deep, restful sleep, but it was difficult as I often had flashbacks from the night in the mountains.

Kamal looked to where the children slept, their heads resting close to one another. The hostesses, with their ruby smiles, had offered sandwiches, tea and an apple. He bit into his sandwich. It tasted wonderful after weeks of stale bread, salty goats cheese and Nutella. He had been surprised to find a product from Australia in a rural Turkish village. He hadn't eaten any fruit since leaving Iran and was saving his apple for last. He hadn't done that since he was a child. He smiled to himself.

They would soon be in Istanbul. There they would be handed over to the local authorities. As soon as they got settled, he had to visit the people at the address given to him by Haales. He wondered if they'd be surprised to see him — alive. Bastards.

The next thing he had to do was collect their passports from the local police. Then he had to figure out a way to travel to the Australian Embassy in Ankara to get their visas. In his breast pocket, he still had the cigarette pack with the name and number Khosro had given the Adliehs. Maybe that man could help him. At least for the next few hours he could pretend he was a tourist, travelling with his family. He rested his head against the seat, closed his eyes and crunched his apple.

At Istanbul, there was some confusion as to which authorities we were to be handed over to. The officers made call after call, trying to figure out where we were meant to go. After dragging us from one end of the airport to the other and back again, they suggested we wait for them in a coffee shop. One of them stayed with us while the other ran back and forth. We ordered black, weak tea and ice-cream, watching an episode of Laurel and Hardy with detached amusement.

Finally, we were ushered into a van and deposited outside Hotel 3M. The hotel was a highrise beside the freeway, not far from the Atatürk Bridge that linked Asia and Europe. The officers seemed to be in a hurry to leave and gave us a hasty goodbye, shaking hands with Dad.

Upstairs, the first thing Nina told Kamal she wanted to do was call home. Nina listened as her grandmother, Aziz, cried on the phone. 'In all my eighty years of life, no one has ever played such a trick on me.'

Eshrat Mamman told them that Jalal and Nasser had gone to Haales's house and Jalal, in his police uniform, had threatened to expose them. Haales's wife swore on her kids' lives that Kamal and his family were all right and being held at the police station in Agri. She also said that Esmat was in Agri and was not pleased with Kamal for naming them.

Fuck him, thought Kamal. The bastard took our money and practically handed us over to the Turkish authorities.

Kamal called Mahin, who cried when she heard his voice. Mamman had gone into a shock when Jalal had told them about the escape. When she took the phone her voice was fragile. Nothing could console her that she was not going to see her eldest son again.

Nina replaced the receiver and sat cross-legged on the bed with her head in her hands. Kamal knew it was hard for her to speak to her family, to hear the pain and anguish in their voices, and to know she was permanently separated from them. He rubbed her back which felt bonier over the past two weeks.

'Now that they have heard from us, they'll be able to cope better,' Nina said.

'Why don't you take a long hot shower?' he suggested, hoping it would take her mind off her family.

She nodded and wiped her face with the back of her hand. She sniffed loudly as she collected her cleanser, walked into the bathroom and gently closed the door behind her. It would be the first time in over two weeks that she could enjoy privacy and the feel of hot running water over her body.

Kamal turned to Behrooz, rubbing his hands hard against one another. 'I don't know about you, but I would kill for a beer.'

A few minutes later there was a light tap on the door. Kamal opened it to find a waiter carrying four cold bottles of beer with frosted glasses. Kamal stared at the tray in disbelief as the waiter carried it to the table; not fully trusting this luxury was for real. He tipped the waiter generously.

Behrooz picked up one of the bottles with the enthusiasm of a child opening their first birthday present after years of being denied any. He raised it towards Kamal 'in good health', and then took a long drink. His Adam's apple moved up and down quickly as he drained the bottle. Kamal followed, the cold beer tingling his throat.

'Aaah,' he said after emptying the bottle, 'that was the best beer I've ever tasted.'

Behrooz laughed and nodded his head in agreement. They sat side by side on the bed with their legs stretched out in front of them, sipping their second beer and enjoying every sinful, delicious minute of it.

After Behrooz left for his room, Kamal walked over to one of the windows facing the other rooms in the motel. Some of the curtains were drawn, which he thought strange for this time of day. He stayed at the window, lost in his thoughts until he noticed a man and woman entering one of the rooms. The man was much older than the woman who was slowly undressing. The man also undressed but first took some money out of his wallet and placed it on the bedstand next to the bed.

'What are you doing by the window?' Nina had just walked out of the shower and had a towel wrapped around her wet hair.

Kamal drew the curtains. 'I don't think this is a proper place for us to stay.'

'We have no choice. You told me yourself the police officers warned us that we have to stay here. Otherwise we could be sent back.'

Kamal's eyebrows drew into a large crease as he told Nina what he had just seen. 'We have to make sure the children are never out of our sight.'

I was surprised by how many soldiers, rifles in hand, lined the streets of Istanbul. I was used to militia and guns but only in the context of enforcing the new Islamic laws. I stared openly at girls with mini skirts and high heels. The shops carried brightly coloured clothes that accentuated the female body rather than hiding it. In the first few days in Istanbul I remained in the same clothes we had escaped in, too frightened and ill at ease to try on sleeveless shirts. For the past couple of years, I had spent a lot of time cheating the hejab: pulling out the odd strand of hair, wearing my scarf loosely, and stealing brief moments of conversation or eye contact with the neighbourhood boys. All the time being wary that everything I did or said could be scrutinised and punished. It was overwhelming to see the way women in Istanbul took their freedom for granted.

Mum and Dad were trying hard to make our stay in Istanbul feel like a holiday, taking us sightseeing, shopping and to the beach. Dad got a haircut in the first week of our stay there. We were shocked by how grey he'd become recently. Mum sat at the edge of the bed and cried, rocking herself back and forth. Dad tried to comfort her, joking about his grey hair. But even though he was laughing his eyes were sunken and there was sadness in them.

Every night we went down to the lobby to watch the World Cup. The hotel was packed with other Iranians who had also escaped. Their tales in the hands of smugglers made us feel lucky we'd been caught at the border. One family had almost starved for two weeks while they'd travelled across Turkey and been made to pay exorbitant prices for old scraps of food. Another group was told to wait in a mill, where they stayed for twenty-four hours without food or water before deciding to try and find a village by themselves. Some escaped from Iran with nomads and their herds of sheep, covering their bodies with sheepskin.

Even though my parents were treating us to a holiday in Istanbul, I could still feel tension in both of them. They still spoke in hushed tones and I heard Dad say that somehow he needed to go to Ankara.

In Turkey, Iranians own police stations

Kamal sat at the foot of the bed, flicking the lid of the cigarette packet back and forth. Flick and shut. Flick and shut.

The last few days had been hard for him. First, the episode with the empty suitcases. Before leaving Iran, Kamal had given two suitcases to Haales to take with him across the border to Turkey. Haales had charged him a hefty fee for it. A few days after arriving in Istanbul, Kamal, along with Behrooz, went to the address Haales had given him. The bags that were handed back to Kamal had their locks broken and hardly weighed anything. Kamal knew Nina had packed them full with clothes, but he decided not to say anything. He and Behrooz had ridden back to the motel in silence.

Flick and shut.

The experience at the police station to get their documents back was even worse. The place was packed with Iranian refugees, most of whom were waiting with their kids. An angry officer sat behind a desk. Kamal approached him and the officer gave him a disgusted look. 'Is there no end to these Iranian motherfuckers?' he said in Turkish.

Kamal was taken aback by the man's offensive language. '*Efendi,*' he spoke in Turkish, 'my name is Dastyari and my documents have been sent here from Agri.'

'Take a seat,' the officer grunted.

Kamal and Behrooz did, joining the others who were crowded around the waiting area. Every few hours a name was called and a family vacated a spot on the floor only to be quickly replaced by another.

Kamal and Behrooz waited there all that day and the following two days before their names were called and their passports handed back. The officer who processed their forms treated them with contempt and it took all his will for Kamal to remain silent.

Flick and shut.

Every time he flicked the cigarette packet open he saw the name and number he had scribbled on the inside cover. He pressed at his temples. The commander and the sergeant had both warned him not to leave Istanbul.

Kamal flicked the packet open and stared at the number again. He reached for the phone, dialled the first few digits, hesitated and hung up. It was probably best not to call this number from the room phone. He slipped on his new shoes, he'd had to throw out the pair he'd left Iran with, and walked out the door. He punched the down arrow on the lift impatiently several times.

Out in the street, he found an empty phone booth and squeezed himself in. He inserted a few coins in the slot and dialled the number.

'Allo,' a man's voice answered, deep and guttural.

Kamal hesitated. His throat felt like sandpaper. What if this man turned him over to the authorities?

'Allo?' the voice came again. This time, sounding impatient.

Kamal asked in Turkish to speak to the man whose name he had scribbled on the packet.

'Don't know such a person,' the man said and hung up.

Kamal felt light-headed and pressed his hand against the booth to steady himself. He patted his jacket for more coins and dialled the number again.

The phone rang for a long time. Just when he thought it would not be answered, it was picked up again.

'Allo.' It was the same man.

'Khosro gave me your name,' Kamal said quickly in Farsi. 'He said you're the kind of man who can fix things.'

There was silence at the other end. Kamal was worried the man would hang up again.

'What's your name?' the man asked.

'Elahi,' Kamal lied. No need for the man to know his real identity.

'Where are you staying?'

'At 3M.'

'I'll meet you at the lobby tonight during the World Cup game.'

Kamal panicked. 'It's really crowded, how will I find you?'

'What are you wearing?'

Kamal told him.

'I'll find you.' And with a click the phone went dead.

In the evenings a small black-and-white television was rolled out in the foyer of the hotel, and guests gathered to watch it. During the World Cup finals there was only standing room.

Mum and I went downstairs early to watch *Dallas*. Aside from our family, there were men drinking alone or in groups of twos and threes. Some were hiding behind the cloud of their cigarette smoke. The man behind the counter ran a brown rag across it. Mum eyed the men suspiciously as she led us to an empty table where we could watch the television clearly. The plastic covering on the pink upholstery made a squeaking sound as we sat down.

Just then a woman walked in. She was the most glamorous woman I had ever seen. She wore a red, wrap-around dress that clung to her body, accentuating her small waist. Her thick dark hair cascaded about her face and shoulders. She stood at the doorway scanning the room and found an empty table close to the television. Once at the table she pulled out a cigarette from her handbag, lit it, took a deep drag as her eyes circled the room and its occupants with an air of indifference.

One of the men drinking alone at a nearby table took his drink and walked over to her table. She did not object to him joining her. The man smiled nervously. He emptied his glass in a single gulp, hesitated as if making his mind up on something, and then leaned over to whisper something in her ear. She nodded, took one last drag from her cigarette and stubbed it out. She then reached into her handbag, pulled out a pen, grabbed a napkin from its holder and scribbled on it. Without looking at the man, she stood and walked towards the door.

As she approached our table her steps slowed down. I looked away embarrassed that I'd been caught staring. But she wasn't looking at me. She was looking at Behzad. Her eyes held the tenderness I had seen in my mum's eyes when she looked at our baby photos. Her dark eyes looked misty as she quickened her steps and headed towards the lifts.

The man at her table looked down at the napkin, folded it and put it in his pocket. Then he too got up and left in the direction she had just gone.

On the television screen the credits for *Dallas* rolled by.

West Germany was playing against France for a chance at the final. The lobby was packed, and Kamal stood at the back. The kids were sitting huddled on either side of Nina. Behrooz had left a few days ago for Sydney. Kamal had felt a tinge of sadness and envy as he'd watched Behrooz board his plane. For the past few weeks Behrooz had replaced his friends and brothers as his closest male companion and confidant. He was deep in thought over Behrooz when he felt a light tap on his shoulder.

Kamal turned to face a man in his mid-thirties, with a thick moustache and light brown eyes. The man wore a khaki jacket and faded blue jeans.

'Elahi?' The man asked.

It took a moment for Kamal to recall that was the name he had given on the phone. He nodded and shook the man's hand. The man stood next to him, pretending to watch the game. He had pulled out a set of worry beads and proceeded to count them between his fingers. The room was very noisy and Kamal had to lean closer to hear him.

'What is it that you need?'

'I need a ticket to Ankara. I'm not permitted to travel outside Istanbul.'

'I'll get you Turkish credentials and a bus ticket. It will cost you fifty US dollars.'

The crowd cheered when West Germany made an attempt at a goal.

'Do you know where Hotel Hilton is?'

Kamal nodded.

'Meet me there on the night of the final.' The man's face became animated. 'They will be bringing out a colour television there. It should be interesting.'

The World Cup final was between Italy and West Germany. We had arrived at the Hotel Hilton early to find ourselves a good spot. Most of the seats were already taken. There was a festive atmosphere in the air and football was the main topic of conversation. The colour television was wheeled into the room to great applause. Everyone stared at its blank screen with much anticipation. We watched the hotel stewards as they fiddled with wires. Soon there was a small crowd gathered around the set, offering their advice as to where and when it should be switched on.

Dad was unusually quiet. He kept pacing the room, straining his neck as if looking for someone. I had to ask him three times for a Coke before he ordered me one. He got a seat for Mum. Behzad and I sat at the foot of the chair. The crowd kept pouring in. Two extra fans that were brought in did little to ease the suffocating feeling of so many people packed next to one another. After protests and much jeering from the crowd, the hotel management decided to turn on the television.

They flicked the switch. The screen burst into an explosion of colour. The crowd cheered. Then, just as quickly, the screen flickered and disappeared to a dot as if swallowed back into itself. The manager shouted at the steward. The steward in turn shouted at his junior assistant. And, as before, a crowd gathered around the set, giving advice and talking over one another. It was a scene straight out of an Abbott and Costello movie. I stood to stretch my legs which were starting to get numb under me. As I did I saw Dad standing in the corner. I waved but he looked straight through me. He seemed to be in a conversation with a man in a khaki jacket.

The crowd pressed forward. Many were getting agitated. The hotel manager tried to calm them as the television was wheeled away. The air was thick with heat and body odour. The set was wheeled back again with extra power cords. After some confusion, a lot of toing-and-froing between staff, and much jeering from the restless crowd, it was switched back on. The crowd cheered as it came to life. The game had already started.

From where he stood, Kamal had a good viewpoint to the entry and most of the lobby, yet he had not noticed the man as he slipped quietly next to him.

'Do you have my money?' he spoke so quietly that Kamal almost did not hear him through all the noise.

'I do. Do you have my ticket?'

The man nodded his head slightly. He was wearing his khaki jacket despite the heat. He slipped his hand inside his breast pocket, pulled out an envelope and handed it to Kamal. Kamal checked the contents.

'You must not be caught with these. I will see you in two days at the bus depot at midnight for the last bus to Ankara.'

Kamal pulled the money out of his jeans and handed it over to him.

'How did you get into this business?' Kamal asked, trying to make light conversation.

The man shrugged his shoulders and smiled. 'In America Iranians own gas stations. In Turkey we own police stations.'

Italy scored and the lobby erupted in a great cheer. Kamal turned to watch the replay. When he turned back again, the man had gone.

The Australian Embassy

The bus station was almost deserted. Kamal ran his hand over
his chin and felt the prickling beard against his palm. He had
decided not to shave. He had walked by the depot yesterday
and studied the dress of the travellers. They were mainly poorer
families and villagers. The men's faces were weather-beaten
and unshaven. Kamal wore his jeans and a crumpled shirt
buttoned to the neck. In the bag he carried, he had packed a
new grey suit, shirt, new tie, new pair of shoes, change of
underwear, bottle of Coke and a sandwich Nina insisted he
should take at the last minute. The letter with the pin number
for their visas was folded neatly inside the passports, tucked
down his jeans. Kamal leaned against the wall at the allotted
terminal taking deep drags on his cigarette, his face disappearing behind a cloud of smoke.

The doors to the bus opened and the driver called out to
the passengers to get their tickets ready. Kamal checked his

watch: 11.45 pm. The bus would be leaving in fifteen minutes but his contact had not shown up with his Turkish ID. He took a step back to allow a few passengers to press through. He searched the crowd. A few minutes later all the passengers had boarded the bus.

The driver called out for any last passengers in a thick, raspy voice.

Where the hell was he? Kamal's eyes darted around the deserted depot.

The last call. The bus driver gave a quick look towards Kamal, shrugged and turned to board his bus.

Kamal's throat went dry.

'*Efendi!*' It was a man's voice coming from the other side of the bus. '*Dur, efendi! Dur.*' The sound of running shoes heading towards them. It was Kamal's contact coming around the bus shouting out 'Stop'. He slowed down when he turned the corner, walking towards the driver with his hand across his chest and smiling broadly. He pumped the driver's hand. Without letting go, he spoke in a low voice so that the driver had to lean closer. When he finally let go of the driver's hand, Kamal noticed the Turkish liras exchanged in the handshake. The man then walked casually towards Kamal, handing him his fake Turkish ID and a return ticket.

'Sit next to the driver and don't talk to anyone. If you do get into any trouble, you have never heard of my name.' His voice was cold and matter-of-fact. He pumped Kamal's hand once and disappeared into the darkness.

Kamal sat by himself behind the driver with his forehead pressed against the window.

The bus rolled into the outskirts of Ankara as morning was breaking. The cabin was silent with only the murmur of a few passengers who, like Kamal, had not managed to sleep, and the hum of the engine. Thankfully, it had not been a long journey. But the seats were uncomfortable and Kamal's back ached. He sat up and stretched. They had stopped at two checkpoints. At each one military men had boarded the bus, flashing their lights into passengers' sleepy faces. Kamal had pretended he was asleep. He'd heard the men ask the driver if Kamal was travelling alone. He had not understood fully what the driver's response was, something about him visiting his sick mother who was dying. It seemed to have satisfied the militia and they had left him alone.

Outside, Ankara was waking up to a clear, warm summer day. The bus driver had begun singing to himself. His head rocked from side to side as he hummed the chorus. Kamal recognised the tune as a popular Turkish song and found himself humming to it.

The bus rolled into the main terminal in Ankara shortly after 6 am. Kamal waited until everyone had departed. The driver was busy helping his few passengers with their luggage and Kamal headed for the taxi terminal.

He walked out of the modern air-conditioned terminal clutching his brown carry bag. A small group of taxi drivers were clustered together on the other side of the road. They stopped talking when they saw the travellers coming, each running to grab a passenger who looked like they might tip the best. Kamal, with his dirty clothes and unshaven face, was not approached. A few taxis drove away with their passengers. The couple that were left behind resumed their conversations.

Kamal crossed the road.

'*Avustralya Ambessy Lutfen,*' he said.

The driver gave Kamal a once-over with his eyes, snorted and resumed his conversation.

'How much?' Kamal asked, tapping the driver on the shoulder.

'You don't look like you could afford it.'

'How much?' Kamal said in a raised voice.

'You're not from around here. Where's your accent from?' the taxi driver asked.

'Australia!' Kamal got into the backseat and slammed the door shut. 'Now let's go.'

Kamal got out into the empty street and paid the taxi driver, tipping him generously.

'You're wasting your time here, *efendi*. It looks deserted now, but in a couple of hours there will be so many people in front of that gate, you'll be lucky if you don't get crushed.'

Balling his fingers around the straps of his bag, Kamal walked down to the tall iron gates. Two soldiers stood in the shade of their guardhouse casting a casual eye over the few men who had already started to gather in front of the gate. The unassuming sign by the side of the gate read in bold black letters, first in English and then in Turkish: 'The Australian Embassy — open weekdays between 8.30 am and 12.30 pm'.

Kamal checked his watch. It was 7 am. He still had time to wash and change his clothes. He had noticed a barbershop further up the street and headed back towards it.

'*Buyuruz, efendi,*' the barber greeted him warmly.

Kamal ran his fingers along his unshaved face. 'I need a wash, a shave and a place to change my clothes.'

'Well, come on in,' the barber beckoned him. 'Don't just stand there. Before you know it, those gossiping women from across the street will be saying that old Hassan has forgotten his hospitality,' he said laughingly.

Inside the small barbershop it was hot and humid. A large fan turned lazily in the corner. There was a hint of brewed tea in the midst of soap and rosewater cologne.

'A traveller are you?' Hassan asked as he placed a hot towel across Kamal's face. 'You have come to the right place, my son. Hassan will make you feel like new again.' His index finger popped into the air like an exclamation mark.

Hassan was an old, jovial man with a full head of white hair. He took unhurried steps across his small shop, stopping often to brew tea for himself and his guests, as he liked to call his customers.

An hour later Kamal stepped out into the street, clean shaven and wearing his brand new suit. He looked down at his suit and smoothed out an imaginary crease from his pants. In his breast pocket he carried the passports and pin numbers for his family's visas.

Kamal turned to give a last wave to Hassan who was busy brewing a fresh pot of tea for his next customer. Kamal had offered him a small amount of money to hold his bag for him, but Hassan had refused, pretending to be offended with exaggerated gestures.

'*Efendi*...you insult me. I will hold your bag in the back, safe till you come back.'

The street had come alive in the past hour and now it was bustling. Vendors lined the street calling over the voices of one another, enticing the pedestrians to stop at their stalls. Kamal walked slowly amongst them, stopping to buy a *piroshke* from one. He felt refreshed despite a sleepless night travelling and was optimistic about the day.

As he got closer to the embassy, he was shocked to see the crowd had grown to be five people deep. People were shouting and pushing one another, pleading with the guards to let them through. The guards, accustomed to such scenes, ignored them.

Once he was at the gate Kamal tried a few times in vain to grab the attention of the guards. But the crowd was too thick and noisy. He tried calling out in English, but his voice was drowned out. He took a few steps back to regroup and think clearly. He suddenly remembered he had a business card from Andrew. He quickly pulled his wallet out and started to look through it. The card was a little damaged from when he had fallen in the river, but it had to do. Holding the card above his head, in a clear authoritative voice he called into the crowd in English, 'Please let me through. I have an appointment... Excuse me, madam, I need to get through. Thank you... That's right, I have an appointment and I have to pass.'

The crowd parted reluctantly, letting him through, and then quickly closed behind him. Kamal was panting by the time he got to the gates. He straightened his tie, squared his shoulders and looked the guard straight in the eye.

'Andrew Fallen is expecting me,' he said in a clear voice.

'What's your name, sir?'

Kamal told him. The guard went into the guardhouse and placed a call. Kamal's stomach twisted and turned inside. Beads of sweat gathered along his browline. He quickly wiped them away with his index finger. After a brief conversation, the guard hung up the phone.

'Mr Fallen's secretary says there is no appointment for you.'

Kamal pretended to be shocked. 'Well, there must be a misunderstanding. I've travelled all the way from Istanbul and it's very important that I should see Andrew.' Kamal purposely used the first name to show an intimacy in their friendship.

'I'm sorry, sir. I can't let you in.'

Kamal fought hard to keep his composure despite the screaming inside his head. 'This is outrageous! I made my appointment a week ago and have travelled six hours to get here.'

From behind, the crowd pressed against him. They had started to push, throwing him momentarily off balance.

'Call him again.' He shouted to be heard over the crowd. 'Speak to Andrew himself this time. I'm sure he will see me.' Kamal knew this was a big gamble. He had not seen Andrew since their interview in Tehran. But they had got on well and Kamal was desperate.

The guard returned to the guardhouse and made another telephone call. This time the conversation was longer. It seemed like an eternity before the guard returned. He had a set of keys in his hands.

Kamal could hardly believe it when he was let through the gates. The guard gave him instructions as to how to get to Andrew's office.

Andrew met Kamal at the front of his office with an outstretched hand and a warm smile.

'Kamal, how are you? I see you have caused quite a commotion outside.' The two men shook hands. 'I'm glad you've made it safely to Turkey.'

'It's been an ordeal. But for now we're just keen to get our visas stamped in our passports and start a new life in Australia.'

Andrew ushered Kamal into his office. It was a modest room with the flag of Australia and a picture of the Queen on the wall. On one side there was a shelf, stacked neatly with books. On his desk was a picture of a woman with a baby in her arms, smiling happily into the camera.

Andrew motioned for Kamal to take the seat opposite him. The secretary walked in with a tray of coffees and a plate of biscuits. She placed them on the desk between the two men. Andrew took the passports and pin numbers from Kamal.

'I'll try to rush these through to be ready for you to collect tomorrow.'

'No, Andrew,' Kamal shook his head, 'I'm afraid they need to be done today.'

'But that's impossible. It —'

'Andrew, I have to be back in Istanbul tonight.' Then in a softer voice, 'Before I'm missed by anyone. Do you understand what I mean?'

Andrew nodded. After a long pause he continued. 'You might have to wait for a little while.'

'I have to catch the midday bus. I have to get back to Nina and the kids.'

'I'll see what I can do.'

It was 11.30 am. Kamal had thirty minutes to get a taxi across the city to the bus station, get changed and catch the bus back to Istanbul with the same driver. He could not afford to get caught. It seemed he had been in the waiting room for an eternity. He had busied himself with the *Sydney Morning Herald* newspapers. They were a few days old, but he had enjoyed reading them, especially the sports pages. It would be good to follow cricket again, he'd enjoyed it when he'd lived in England. This Dennis Lillee should be very entertaining to watch.

'Kamal.' Andrew's voice had brought his thoughts back to the room. He'd quickly risen to his feet. Andrew was smiling and in his hands were the passports.

'I hope your trip to Sydney will be less eventful than your journey so far.'

When Kamal walked through the embassy gates the sun was high in the sky. The air was warm and still. It reminded Kamal of the day in the Caspian Sea when he had first heard the news of demonstrations in Tehran. There was no wind that day either. Ironic how he should be thinking about that day now.

It had taken all his effort not to run to Andrew and snatch the passports off him. But now, outside, he was running up the street to the barbershop, still clutching the passports. He ran into the shop, startling Hassan who offered him a tea.

While Hassan slowly retrieved his bag, Kamal flagged down a taxi. He thanked Hassan and got into the taxi.

'I'll give you fifty liras extra if you get me to the bus terminal in ten minutes,' Kamal dangled the notes in front of the driver and saw his eyes sparkle.

In the taxi he stripped off his jacket and tie, and unbuttoned his shirt. At the terminal he paid the driver who had committed several traffic offences to get him there with a few minutes to spare. He wasted precious minutes working out which depot his bus departed from, and had changed into his jeans in the men's toilets under the shocked gaze of other travellers. He checked his watch: noon. He was going to miss his bus. He started sprinting. His chest heaved with every breath and his legs burned.

'If I make it to Australia, I will definitely give up smoking.'

In the distance he saw the bus driver boarding the bus. The bus rattled as the engine burst into life.

Please, dear God. Don't let him go without me.

He had almost reached the bus. '*Efendi! Efendi, dur!*'

The bus moved forward.

'*Dur! Dur!*' he shouted again for the bus to stop. He didn't think his lungs and legs would hold up any longer. He stopped. Tears stung the back of his eyes. He was so close.

The bus suddenly stopped and the doors folded open.

Inside, Kamal rested his head against the seat in relief. He pulled out the passports and opened them. He traced his fingers along the outline of the visa. He had pulled his family out of Iran against all odds.

Kamal tucked the passports at the bottom of his bag. All the emotions of the past few months came rushing over him like a spring shower.

Alone, with his face pressed to the window, Kamal wept freely.

Sydney

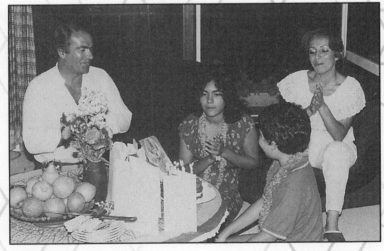

Welcome to Sydney

Kamal looked to where Nina and the kids slept. He watched her chest as it rose and fell in a slow rhythm. Her face muscles were relaxed. The new creases around her eyes and lips were the only signs of the strain she had silently endured the last few months. The kids, on either side of her, slept with their faces pressed against her arms, breathing her in.

The rising sun crept through the slit between the blind and window, casting a warm glow across their faces. Kamal reached over to pull down the blind. He looked out. Below them Australia stretched out, its red earth vibrant and vast. He imagined kangaroos hopping in packs like the pictures in the *National Geographic*.

He smiled and pulled the blind all the way down. He relaxed in his seat and rested his head back. He had not slept well. Flashes of the night on the mountains, the gunfire, and their time in the jail still haunted him. In Hong Kong, where they had planned to spend a night, the authorities had refused them entry, forcing them to sleep on the hard plastic chairs until the next flight to Sydney. A deep shame had washed over him as he felt other travellers staring as the police escorted them away.

He picked up a copy of the *TIME* magazine the stewardess had given him. He wanted to push the unpleasant thoughts away, drown them. He stared at the cover. Two years ago Ayatollah Khomeini was on the front cover as *TIME*'s 'Man of the Year'. He flicked through the pages. There was a review of an Australian film *Gallipoli*. He read the review. The Americans needed subtitles. He frowned – how bizarre.

A little while later, the plane lights came on and the stewardesses began preparing the cabin. Nina blinked and opened her eyes. She woke the kids with the stir of her hand and a gentle kiss on their foreheads.

Soon there was an announcement on the speakers.

'This is the captain speaking. We have begun our descent into Sydney. Crew please prepare the plane for landing.'

I pulled up the blind. We were still flying above the cotton-candy clouds. Some other passengers were also looking out their windows. But most continued to read or listen to their walkmans. The plane rattled slightly as it plunged into the clouds. Droplets of water clung to the window, blurring visibility.

Then all of a sudden the clouds were gone and Sydney lay before us. The houses with their red tin roofs lined the streets in formation. It was the morning of 8 August 1982 and Sydney-siders were waking up to a cool winter day. None of them knew how extraordinary that day was for us. None of them gave a thought that on that day their population had increased by four Iranian immigrants wanting desperately to start a new life amongst them. None of them celebrated that day with us. In time, maybe we wouldn't either. It would become just another winter day.

The plane circled Sydney and for the first time I saw the harbour. The crescent-shaped Harbour Bridge stood proud above the diamond-studded water. From above, the Opera House looked like a waterlily, slowly unravelling itself to greet the morning sun.

Our new home was beautiful.

The plane landed with a thud. The wheels screeched as they gripped the tarmac, decelerating and finally coming to a complete stop.

'Welcome to Sydney,' the captain's voice boomed over the speakers. Kamal did not hear the rest of it. The three words kept ringing in his ears. It was like a dream he had yet to wake from. A small smile crept across his face.

In customs Kamal showed their passports at every checkpoint. The puffy-eyed immigration officer opened them, lifted his eyes for a few seconds to compare the photos to the four standing in front of him, stamped them, and handed the passports back to Kamal.

'Next,' he called out to the people in the queue.

Kamal and Nina exchanged a look. 'Is that all?' Kamal asked the officer.

'What else were you expecting, mate?' the officer said in a broad nasal accent.

Kamal ignored the impatience of the travellers queuing behind them.

'Where do we go?' he asked. He pushed the passports back at the immigration officer. Maybe the man had not noticed that they were Iranians. Maybe he had missed the exit stamp from Turkey declaring them as illegals and the refusal stamp from Hong Kong.

The officer took the passports, opened them again, checked the visa and handed them back with a smile.

'Anywhere you like, mate,' he said.

Epilogue

It's been over twenty-five years since we crossed illegally into Turkey.

Mum and Dad bought bookshop franchises and a house in the new suburbs of Sydney. Eventually our family members were sponsored and every year another relative was added. Eshrat Mamman stayed for three months and decided to go back to Iran. I only saw her once more when I travelled with my two young sons to visit her when my aunt Soheyla lived in Kansas City.

Mum went back to Iran when Eshrat Mamman was diagnosed with cancer only to get her passport confiscated. It took her eight weeks, a lot of waiting in officials' doorways, and a few greased palms before she was able to get back to Sydney. Dad never went back, he had burnt too many bridges and all those blank pages he had signed on his last day in the office...well, they didn't turn out to his benefit.

Behzad and I have never been back to Iran either. The closest I came was on a flight to London with my husband Mark. It was early in the morning and the cabin was dark. The only light came from sole travellers like me who couldn't sleep, and from the flickering light of the screen.

The oversized silhouette of our plane moved slowly over the Middle East. Iran, the unmistakable shape of a cat, slowly emerged from the corner. It took forty-five minutes to travel across it. During that time the pain in my heart felt like a cold iron claw clasped around my chest, making it difficult to breathe. Images of my childhood flooded my vision: days spent in the safety of my grandmother's arms; the revolution and the war with Iraq; huddled in our basement with the rat-tat-tat of machine guns shredding the night sky; the night on the mountains with my face pressed against the cold dirt; and the nights cramped in the prison cell. All this fell upon me like large droplets of rain. Hot, salty tears streamed steadily down my face. My mouth was slightly open, trying to inhale oxygen through raspy breaths.

Dad had said our images of the past are like old pictures, filed away in our subconscious. Once in a while something reminds us of them and they're pulled out, dusted, looked at and remembered. And in that moment all the pain, the fear and uncertainty rushes back and drowns you before slowly withdrawing back into the corner of your mind, where it remains dormant and waiting. Like an old wound that never quite heals.

I once read a quote by a Greek writer, Euripides, 'There is no greater sorrow on earth than the loss of one's native land.'

When I read that quote I wondered, why would anyone with a seemingly intelligent mind want to uproot their family? Why would they break away the branches of their family tree from the bosom of those who loved and nurtured them? Why would they leave the friends they have shared a lifetime of memories with, and the soil their ancestors have fought for? Why endanger their lives to travel to another corner of the world where, for the rest of their days, they will remain a foreigner with an accent, a refugee, a stranger to their culture?

When I began writing this book, I asked my parents why they did it . . . I expected them to take a few moments to reflect on their thoughts, but their answer was brief and without hesitation.

'A chance for a better life.'

Their decision twenty-five years ago means that my children will never have to know what it is like to wake up at night to the sound of gunfire. They will not have to fear men who would turn on them with guns and irrational ideology when they were meant to protect them.

ABOVE: *(clockwise) Banafsheh, Behzad, Kamal and Nina, 2004*

A note from the author...

I felt a need — rather than a want — to write this book.

A need to give a voice to thousands of refugees who, at great risk to their lives, have fled oppressive regimes or war-torn countries, and are wrongly imprisoned in detention centres.

I want my own children, who may otherwise dismiss the plight of these people, to identify with them through my experiences and not just turn a blind eye.

These refugees are our mothers and fathers, brothers and sisters...ourselves — not just faceless strangers.

Another reason for writing this book was a way of thanking my parents. From the moment Behzad and I were told we were leaving Iran, we placed our complete and unquestioning trust in our parents to keep us safe. It was only when I held my first-born in my arms that I realised what a huge and terrifying responsibility that must have been for them to carry.

ABOVE: *Nicholas, Mark, Dominic and Banafsheh, 2006*

Acknowledgments

I thank my parents whose courage and passion led us to Australia; my beautiful husband Mark and our sons Nicholas and Dominic for their support, patience and belief in me; Artemis Keyhani, whom I will always remain indebted to for her initial readings of my draft layout. I would like to thank the wonderful people at Hachette Livre who made me feel welcome. I would like to thank Bernadette Foley for her belief in me and her immense encouragement and support, and my wonderful editor Deonie Fiford who made sure no detail was overlooked and gave me the support I needed to realise my dream. Finally I would like to thank my friends and extended family for their interest, cheering me on at every stage to make sure I never ever give up.